MILITARY
ENGAGEMENT

MILITARY ENGAGEMENT

Influencing Armed Forces Worldwide to Support Democratic Transitions

VOLUME I
Overview and Action Plan

DENNIS BLAIR

A project of the Council for a Community of Democracies

BROOKINGS INSTITUTION PRESS
Washington, D.C.

ABOUT BROOKINGS

The Brookings Institution is a private nonprofit organization devoted to research, education, and publication on important issues of domestic and foreign policy. Its principal purpose is to bring the highest quality independent research and analysis to bear on current and emerging policy problems. Interpretations or conclusions in Brookings publications should be understood to be solely those of the authors.

Military Engagement: Influencing Armed Forces to Support Democratic Transitions may be ordered from Brookings Institution Press,
1775 Massachusetts Avenue, N.W., Washington, D.C. 20036
www.brookings.edu/press
Telephone: 1-800/537-5487 or 410/516-6956
e-mail: hfscustserv@press.jhu.edu

Library of Congress Cataloging-in-Publication data
Blair, Dennis C.
    Military engagement : influencing armed forces to support democratic transitions / Dennis Blair.
        pages   cm
    Includes bibliographical references and index.
    ISBN 978-0-8157-2505-3 (pbk. : alk. paper)
    1. Armed Forces—Civic action. 2. Armed Forces—Political activity.
3. Democracy. 4. Civil-military relations. 5. Military relations. 6. Politics and war. 7. World politics—21st century. I. Council for a Community of Democracies. II. Title.
    UH720.B53 2013
    322'.5—dc23   2013001646

9 8 7 6 5 4 3 2 1

Typeset in Sabon and Ocean Sans

Composition by Cynthia Stock
Silver Spring, Maryland

For

MARK PALMER
1941–2013

Champion of democracy

Contents

Foreword

Dr. Susilo Bambang Yudhoyono
President, Republic of Indonesia

Indonesia today is recognized as the world's third largest democracy after India and the United States, and one of the most successful transformational stories of the early 21st century. We have come a long way from independence in 1945 to be where we are today: a stable and peaceful democracy; a coherent multi-ethnic nation; a G-20 emerging economy; a regional power with global interests.

The Indonesian armed forces (TNI) have always played a powerful and important role in Indonesia's history. They defeated the colonial powers' attempts to reclaim Indonesia by force after World War II, and they became a formidable political force for many decades since our independence in 1945. In the late 1990s, the TNI made a historic move to begin the process of becoming a professional military and decoupling themselves from politics. As it turned out, this became an important factor for Indonesia's democratic transition which began in 1998. Indeed, of all the national reforms undertaken at the time—constitutional, political, electoral, bureaucratic, financial, legislative, legal, etc.—military reform was among the most swift, far-reaching and decisive.

As the Chief of Staff of the Socio-Political Affairs of the TNI in 1997–1998, and as Chair of the Drafting Committee of TNI Reforms, I was privileged to play my part in designing the blueprint of Indonesia's future military. Significantly, we began this process even before the economic and political turbulences that led to our democratic transition. We read the signs of the time, and decided that it was necessary for the TNI to adapt to a different future by reforming itself. As we charted our path through intense political uncertainty, I was fortunately able to draw from various lessons learned from the experience of other democratic transitions as well as established democracies. I knew that it was critically necessary for the TNI to stay the course and fully support Indonesia's new democracy through trials and tribulations. The Indonesian experience, in my view, serves as a useful reference for other countries undergoing democratic transition today. It is an example that I have actively shared in my discussions with Myanmar's military leaders in recent years, among others.

Admiral Dennis Blair has written an important book on military relations and supporting democratic development. He is well-suited to this task, given that he witnessed some of the transition events examined in the book. As Commander in Chief of the United States Pacific Command, he had visited Indonesia and had constructive discussions with me during important moments of our democratic consolidation. Admiral Blair therefore writes on the subject of military-to-military relations and democratic development with extensive knowledge and well-deserved authority.

With the help of international co-authors, Admiral Blair describes how democratic change has come to many armed forces around the world, and how outside countries can help support that change. Indonesia will do what it can to share our experience with other countries on the often long and difficult road of democratic development, in which armed forces will play a vital role. As Admiral Blair urges, the armed forces of all democratic countries need to work together on this important mission.

February 2013

Acknowledgments

This handbook, and its companion volume, draws its inspiration from late Ambassador Mark Palmer (1941–2013). Ambassador Palmer came up with the original idea for a practical guide for using military engagement to assist democratic development, and he was a constant source of support and advice from the inception of the project two years ago. He has been an inspiration for decades to all who work for democracy, and will be missed. This handbook forms a small part of his enduring legacy.

Several foundations and individuals provided intellectual and financial assistance during the production of this handbook. *Military Engagement* would not have been produced without the support of the Smith Richardson Foundation. A special thanks to Dr. Nadia Schadlow for her guidance throughout the process. Dr. Peter Ackerman, chairman and founder of the International Center on Nonviolent Conflict, provided crucial feedback on the content, specifically with respect to the role of the military during a civil resistance movement. We are grateful to the support of the Taiwan Foundation for Democracy, which made possible a number of case studies. ATK also provided financial support for the project. Thanks to Deloitte for hosting a panel discussion on the handbook and to Joel Cowan and Greg Hunter for their support. Michael Miklaucic,

Hans Binnendijk, and their colleagues at the National Defense University volunteered their ideas, as well as time and efforts to supply images for both volumes. Thanks to Dick Rowson for his efforts and advice on publication. Al Stolberg at the Army War College in Carlisle, Pennsylvania, provided steady advice and review of many drafts along the way. I was also inspired, assisted, and often brought back to reality by conversations and interviews with many former colleagues and new acquaintances around the world. They are too numerous to thank individually, but I am sure they will recognize some of their ideas here.

This project would not have been possible without the outstanding work of the team of regional coordinators and coauthors of the second volume. A special thanks to General Juan Emilio Cheyre and to Dr. Muthiah Alagappa, Ambassador Istavan Gyarmati, General Tannous Mouawad, Dr. Matthew Rhodes, and Dr. Martin Rupiya.

Thanks finally to the Council for a Community of Democracies (CCD) staff for their sponsorship of the project, administrative support, and assistance in the editing and production of the handbook: CCD President Bob LaGamma, Rebecca Aaberg, Chris Brandt, Dan Hollingsworth, Garrett Nada, and Randi Zung.

Introduction:
Influencing Dictatorships
to Become Democracies

This handbook is about the role of armed forces in the support and spread of democracy. Its purpose is to inspire and instruct the ministries of defense and armed forces of the established democracies to make the support of democracy a priority mission. They can and should help enable democratic transitions in countries still governed by authoritarian regimes as well as those that have already started on the road to representative government but have not reached a solid and resilient democratic destination. All the established democracies—in Asia, Europe, and North and South America—have hundreds of points of contact with other armed forces that can serve to strengthen various aspects of democratic development. The long-established democracies—the United States, the United Kingdom, France, and Canada—have links from international activity stretching back many years. Many of the newer democracies—Brazil, Chile, Czech Republic, Ghana, India, Indonesia, Mongolia, Poland, South Africa, and Spain—have recent experiences with their own transitions that are relevant and valuable to other countries starting to democratize. However, in the democratic countries, disparate programs and opportunities are not integrated under a firm policy of support for democratic development: they are not systematic, are generally reactive rather than proactive, do not take on the hard cases—the

strongest dictatorships—and are not coordinated internationally. By addressing these issues, this handbook shows how the
established democracies can take advantage of all their points of
contact and influence to move dictatorships toward democracy.

The approach described here is not about regime change
by military means. It is not about supporting armed freedom
fighters against dictatorships nor about invading authoritarian
countries to establish democracy by force of arms. As explained
in chapter 6, nonviolent democratic transformations in recent
decades have proved far more durable than the armed overthrow of dictatorships. The objective of the recommendations in
this handbook is rather to persuade the armed forces of authoritarian governments that they should not oppose, and should
even favor, peaceful transitions to democratic governments in

Military personnel from the United Kingdom, Australia, Canada, France, and the United States participate in
a Remembrance Day ceremony November 11, 2009. (DoD photo by Staff Sgt. Robert Barney, U.S. Air Force/
Released)

their own countries. They should do so both because it is best for their countries and in the self-interest of the armed forces in which they serve. What is best for a country is a government that enjoys the full support of its people, a representative government following the rule of law—in other words, a democracy. What is in the self-interest of any military force is a democratic system, in which a military officer can be confident that he or she will be defending the people rather than attacking them, be respected for service, have a fair chance of promotion, receive adequate compensation, and be able to retire with honor.

The Armed Forces Matter in Democratic Transitions

The armed forces are one of the most powerful institutions in any country. They have weapons and disciplined personnel, and are organized for taking action. To an extent that is hard for military officers and officials in mature democratic countries to understand, the military leaders of new countries and new governments believe they have both the right and the responsibility to play a decisive role in the political development of their countries. Their independence wars are more recent, military coups have been frequent and not long ago, and few other established institutions have their power and influence within the country. They will often assume or be thrust into a decisive role in a political crisis, and large sectors of society will look to them for leadership and action.

Rarely will a country's armed forces be in the vanguard of a popular movement for democratic reform. It is true that many military coups are proclaimed to have been made in the name of the people and that their leaders often announce that their goal is to restore or establish democracy. Once in power, however, they generally then announce that it will take a period of time to deal with the country's immediate problems before power can be turned over to a democratic government. As that period of time becomes longer and longer, the rulers may exchange their uniforms for business suits, but they generally convince themselves they do not need an election to confirm their own conviction that they are the most qualified candidates to lead the country. This has been the pattern in many African countries when anticolonial military revolutionaries became long-serving dictators. Often it takes another coup or a political crisis to force them from power. However, power has not always corrupted absolutely, and there have been examples of military governments voluntarily relinquishing power: the military regimes in Chile and Brazil in the 1980s sensed growing popular demands for democracy and led the transition process themselves.[1] More recently, the Thai military government turned over power to the party led by the sister of the leader they had deposed months earlier.

The armed forces can suppress most revolts against authoritarian regimes if they decide to support the dictator or party in power. In 1989 the People's Liberation Army cleared Tiananmen Square. In 2009 armed forces of Iran obeyed orders to quell popular protests against the clerical regime, which continues in power to this day. At the time of this writing, the Syrian armed forces continue to follow orders from their dictator to suppress revolt, and President Assad remains in power.

However, the armed forces do not always support their authoritarian leaders when their power is challenged, even authoritarian leaders who appointed and courted them. When there is a political crisis, military leaders make decisions on what they feel is best for their country, their services, and their personal interests. It is not rare for the armed forces to play a positive role in allowing popular movements to overthrow dictators, even if the latter have been in power for a long time and have assiduously courted and controlled their military leaders. In the Philippines in 1983, Indonesia in 1998, Serbia in 2000, and the Ukraine in 2004, the armed forces refused to suppress protesters, in some cases cooperating with them, and allowed the dictators to be overthrown.[2] In 2011 the Tunisian and Egyptian army leaderships decided not to support the Ben Ali and Mubarak regimes against popular protests, and those dictators fell.[3]

The armed forces play an absolutely key role in fostering, allowing, or suppressing democratic movements in authoritarian states. Thus it is very much in the interests of the established democracies to help military leaders in authoritarian or transition countries make the right choices.

Characteristics of Armed Forces under Dictatorships

Dramatic events, like the decisions of military leaders during the Arab Awakening to support their leaders or to turn on them, are the culmination of long-term, complex sets of developments. Military leaders, even in isolated dictatorships, understand that over the long run, a government must have the support of its people. They also understand that military dictatorship—direct military rule of the country—is neither practical nor sustainable in today's world: Myanmar/Burma is only the latest example of a long line of military dictatorships that have tried to turn power over to another, more representative form of government. The only pure military dictatorship today is Fiji, scarcely a trendsetter. Most military officers—though there are plenty of exceptions—believe that the armed forces should act as the defenders of their people, not as the instrument of their repression. The ethos of armed forces and the creed of most of those who serve is patriotic defense of the nation and its people. They are at their best in honing their skills to defend their country against its enemies. Turning weapons against their own people contradicts the fundamental professional convictions of military people. Participation in the brutal political struggle for self-preservation that is the preoccupation of dictatorships is neither the preference nor the skill set of military officers. Many military officers, even in autocratic regimes, often have a general sentiment that some kind of a representative government is ultimately best for their nations.

However, many other circumstances and beliefs cause military leaders and their troops to support autocratic governments as necessary for their countries for the time being—and "the time being" can stretch for decades. Some military leaders are simply thugs who joined for power. For others, self-interest, corruption, and fear play roles. Dictators take care of senior military leaders, especially in poorer countries. At lower ranks, soldiers are rewarded with scarce food in North Korea, and receive regular pay or opportunities for extortion in other impoverished dictatorships. Despots also check their generals' loyalty through independent intelligence services and other informer networks, and they remove and punish harshly those considered unreliable. Even as the overwhelmingly powerful American-led international military coalition was gathering on Iraq's border in 2003, its generals were far more afraid of Saddam Hussein than they were of the military defeat they could see looming.

Beyond these human motivations, however, are other beliefs and convictions. When a country is threatened by social turmoil, especially when supported, or suspected to be supported, from outside the country, a military leader may believe that his first duty is to maintain law and order, fight against foreigners or their surrogates, and support the current government in order to maintain social stability. This was certainly the case for many Latin American military officers who fought against Cuban- and Soviet-supported insurgencies in the 1970s and 1980s. While many of their actions were reprehensible, their basic motivation was understandable.[4] It is easy to believe that reform must be postponed until a more stable time. Military leaders also are influenced or can be manipulated by ethnic and tribal divisions in those countries where identity politics play a major role. It is a rare military officer who will support democratic reform if he believes his ethnic group or tribe will be oppressed or disadvantaged under an unproven democratic system. These considerations play a role in many African countries today.

There are sometimes other core beliefs that are dominant in the values of military leaders. Turkish military officers believe their duty is to safeguard the secular nature of their government. Thai officers believe the king must be respected.

Finally, many military officers honestly believe that their countries are not yet ready for democracy. They feel that the necessary institutions for democracy do not yet exist in their countries: an informed citizenry that will elect competent political leaders, an honest and functional legal system that will protect minority rights and tame corruption, a capable civil service, and a responsible legislature. They believe that until these components of democracy are present, some form of authoritarian government that earns popular support is best for their countries.

The military leaders serving under dictatorships are not automatons programmed to give absolute fealty to despots whom they will defend to the death. They each have a set of beliefs, self-interest, and fears that form their overall attitude to their government and that will govern their actions during political changes. It is important to understand the motivations and interests of officers in autocratic regimes in order to persuade them to support democratic reform and transition.

Democratic Transitions

With all these circumstances and beliefs blocking democratic progress, how are advances made? The regional surveys and case studies in this handbook show that change comes through a combination of events and individuals.

Time and again, democratic transitions have been moved forward by the decisions of individual military officers who understood that it was right for their countries and their military services. In the early years of the United States, George Washington declined to be a proconsul and supported a constitutional democratic form of government. A century and a half later in Turkey, Mustafa Kemal Atatürk used his enormous prestige as the military victor in a war of independence to support the establishment of a democratic form of government for his country.[5] As described later in this handbook, other military leaders have played similar important roles in more recent years. In Senegal General Jean Alfred Diallo in the 1960s established a positive role for the armed forces in his newly independent country that has continued to the present. In Spain in the 1970s, General Gutierrez Mellado was the "irreplaceable initiator of reform" in Spain's transition from the Franco dictatorship. In the 1980s, General Prem Tinsulanonda, as prime minister of Thailand, moved his country toward democracy and voluntarily left the premiership for an elected successor. General Fidel Ramos stepped down after a constitutionally mandated single term as president of the Philippines, declining to support an initiative to change the constitution or to declare martial law. In the 1990s, Staff General Ferenc Vegh, the Hungarian chief of defense, led the reform of the armed forces toward a new democratic role. General Juan Emilio Cheyre, one of the coauthors of the second volume of this handbook, brought the Pinochet era to a close in Chile in 2004 by promulgating a public manifesto committing the Chilean armed forces to service in a democratic society. In Tunisia in 2011, General Rachid Ammar refused orders to use military force to suppress peaceful protests, leading to the end of President Ben Ali's dictatorship.

These individual acts of courage and leadership do not occur in a vacuum. They are based on the education, training, and experiences of individual officers. The generals and admirals in the top leadership positions both influence and are influenced by networks of other officers and military officials, some of whom are dedicated to positive change both in their military services and for their countries. As the case histories in this handbook demonstrate, these reform networks within military services come together and take action primarily based on internal factors. Officers serving authoritarian regimes are often dissatisfied with conditions within their military services—cronyism, corruption, slow promotions, military defeat, and low professionalism—and within the country—corruption, economic adversity, deteriorating security conditions, and succession crises. However, outside influences also play a role: it can be negative if democratic reform is not encouraged or positive if it promotes reform. The policies of outside countries and international organizations and the words and actions of individual foreigners count. Officers and defense officials from the mature democracies can make a difference when they encourage their counterparts to support transitions toward more representative government and assume a role for their forces that is less political and more professional.

Persuading the Guys with the Guns

The armed forces of almost all countries around the world—those of democracies, dictatorships, and transitional states—are in constant contact. A few countries, such as North Korea and Iran, effectively isolate their military officers from outside contact, but they are the exception.[6] Military officers from both democracies and dictatorships participate in exchange programs, and military delegations visit other countries regularly and attend international conferences together. Military units from one country provide training to other countries, and military units train and work together in coalitions in disaster relief and peacekeeping operations around the world.

These military points of contact offer to the armed forces of developed democracies opportunities to influence their

Outside Influences on Democratic Development:
Today's Academic Consensus

Rather than assert the primacy of either international or domestic factors, we argue that their relative causal weight varies across countries and regions. External forces reshape domestic incentives and power distributions, often in ways that are decisive to regime outcomes. However, they do so to varying degrees across cases. In regions with extensive ties to the West (particularly Central Europe and the Americas), international influences were so intense that they contributed to democratization even where domestic conditions were highly unfavorable. In these cases, we concur with those who posit the primacy of international variables. However, where ties to the West were less extensive, post–Cold War international democratizing pressure was weaker, and consequently, domestic factors weighed more heavily. In these cases, regime outcomes are explained primarily by domestic structural variables, particularly the strength of state and governing party organizations.

Quoted from Steven Levitsky and Lucan A. Way, *Competitive Authoritarianism: Hybrid Regimes after the Cold War* (Cambridge University Press, 2010), chapter 2.

counterparts in authoritarian countries. During education and training courses, through rewards and sanctions, and in professional and personal discussions, the military forces of democratic countries can convey by both example and persuasion the advantages that the armed forces of democracies enjoy and encourage their peers to support democratic transitions in their countries.

Influence is most effectively exerted over time through a sustained program of conveying the essential elements and advantages of a democratic system to counterparts in autocratic regimes. Interactions with autocratic regimes—China, Saudi Arabia, Uzbekistan, Venezuela, Vietnam, Zimbabwe—will differ from those with countries in transition—Cambodia,

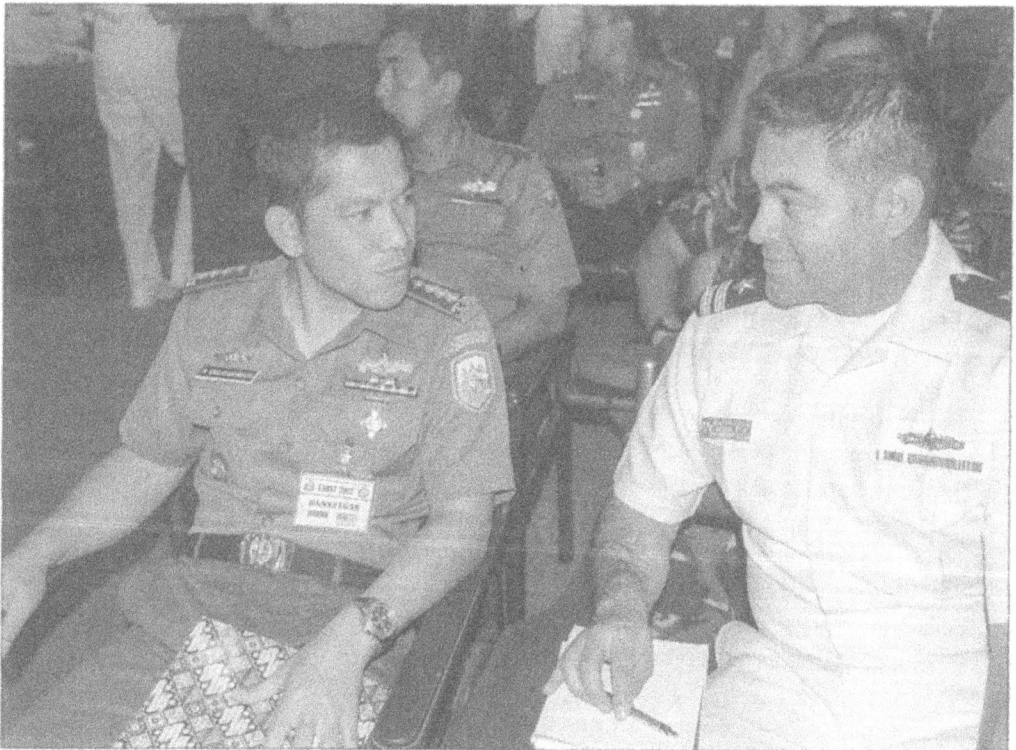

U.S. Navy and Indonesian Navy junior officers conferring duing bilateral exercises. (DoD photo by Lt. Fernando Rivero, U.S. Navy/Released)

Ecuador, Egypt, El Salvador, Kazakhstan, Nigeria, Serbia, Sri Lanka. The way in which messages are delivered is crucial, according to several of the coauthors of the second volume of this handbook who have been on the receiving end of efforts to convince them to promote democracy in their countries. If messages are delivered in an arrogant, condescending, insensitive

The Democracy "Elevator Speech"

The following is a list of points that an officer from a democratic country can convey in a short conversation with a counterpart from an autocratic country:

➤ Democracy is spreading throughout the world. We are in the midst of the fourth wave of democratic transitions.

➤ Democracy in different forms is the aspiration of people on all continents: Africa, Asia, Eastern Europe, the Middle East, and South America.

➤ No regime can remain in power if it is not supported by its people.

➤ Dictatorships will one day call on their armed forces to betray their oaths and will order them to use force against their own citizens.

➤ The loyalty of the armed forces should be to the people and their chosen representatives, not some self-chosen person or party.

➤ Armed forces in democracies serve only to defend their people and will never be required to use force against them.

➤ Service members in democracies are respected, adequately compensated, fairly promoted, and retire with honor.

➤ Democracies field the most capable armed forces in the world.

➤ The military heroes that history remembers have acted not to oppress their people but to defend them.

manner, they will be counterproductive. If they are delivered in a way that is sensitive to the history, conditions, and aspirations of the officer serving in an autocratic or transitional country, then they can have impact.

When political crises occur, advanced democracies must exert influence in a more intense and coordinated fashion. Different countries will have different types and degrees of influence. Personal contacts among military officials and officers in democratic countries and military leaders in the autocratic and transitional countries will be important. The officer or official in the democracy with the most knowledge, friendships, and influence within the country in transition may have to be called from another assignment to work on the transition. Timing will be crucial, as will be up-to-date knowledge about the situation within the country in transition, quick decisions within the democratic countries about their policies toward transitions, and a rapid exchange of information among the democracies so that all their efforts are mutually reinforcing.

Influencing Armed Forces in Dictatorships and Helping Armed Forces in Transition

This handbook provides practical recommendations for using military relations to promote democratic development. Most of its analysis and recommendations are aimed at influencing countries with autocratic governments. In the latest survey by

The Democracy Mission

➤ Persuade the armed forces of autocratic countries to support, or at least not to oppose, democratic transitions in their country.

➤ Work with the armed forces of countries transitioning to democracy to establish the policies, authorities, and practices of the military services in a democratic system of government.

Freedom House, 47 of the world's 194 countries were dictatorships, governing 34 percent of the world's population.[7] The "worst of the worst" are Equatorial Guinea, Eritrea, North Korea, Saudi Arabia, Somalia, Sudan, Syria, Turkmenistan, and Uzbekistan, closely followed by Belarus, Chad, China, Cuba, and Laos. These countries make no pretensions of a commitment to democracy and expect their armed forces to control their populations as much as to defend them. Yet the armed forces of many of these countries have contact with the armed forces of democratic countries. These contacts offer opportunities to plant and nurture the idea that their countries would be better if they were democratic and that their military services would be more honored, better remembered, and better aligned with their ethos if their governments made the transition to democracy. Political crises will come to these countries, and during those crises, military influences can be used to support democratic outcomes.

In addition to putting dictatorships on the path toward democracy, the established democracies must also help other countries that have already begun reform programs. There are fifty-eight countries that Freedom House classifies as "Partly Free."[8] These countries, and several others that are classified "Free," have governments that are democratic in their form and aspirations but are not fully established democracies. They generally welcome contact with the armed forces of the mature democracies to strengthen their own armed forces, including their commitment to democracy. NATO, for example, has an extensive program of country partnerships and regularly conducts exercises with the military forces of a number of these countries; invites them to meetings, seminars, and educational institutions in NATO countries; and sends training teams to assist them in areas such as military education and defense budgeting. An informal network of mature democracies, led by the United Kingdom and France, and with many other participating countries and nongovernmental organizations, such as the Swiss-sponsored Democratic Control of the Armed Forces, assists many African countries in transition through a process called Security System Reform. Expert advisers provide knowledge and training across the full range of military functions needed for democratic governance. Although these programs are not the primary focus of this handbook—there are other excellent resource materials available—they are very important, ensuring that countries that have started the move toward democratic governance do not lose ground because their armed forces have not developed the characteristics congruent with a democratic system.

In summary, the militaries of democracies around the world have literally hundreds of opportunities to influence counterparts in autocratic or transitioning countries. Taking advantage of these opportunities to persuade their peers of the national, military, and personal advantages of democratic governance is one of the most important contributions that democratic armed forces can make to the security of their own countries and to a peaceful future world.

2

What the Armed Forces Look Like in a Democracy

Officers who serve in the armed forces of long-established democracies generally take for granted the laws and customs that govern their actions within their countries. They would never think of participating in political activity in uniform or questioning the authority of the legislature to cut their budgets. Having grown up with these customs, military officers in democracies often have little knowledge of the origins, rationale, or importance of democratic civilian authority. If officers in democracies are to convince their counterparts in autocratic systems of the superiority of military service in a democratic system, they must understand fundamental principles and the different forms they can take in different countries.

The best single statement of the characteristics of the armed forces of a democracy is the December 1994 *Code of Conduct on Politico-Military Aspects of Security,* adopted in Budapest, Hungary, by the Organization for Security and Cooperation in Europe.[1] This code of conduct pledges the member nations, currently fifty-five in number, to use force only in accordance with the charter of the United Nations, and then it goes on to set forth the principles under which security services will be established and controlled. It states, "Each participating State will at all times provide for and maintain effective guidance to and control of its military, paramilitary and security forces by constitutionally established authorities vested with democratic legitimacy."[2]

Just as democracy itself is more than elections, the role of the armed forces in a democracy is more than "civilian control of the military."[3] After all, civilian dictators often control their military forces effectively. In a democracy, the armed forces are established by the fundamental laws of the country—its constitution or legal code. Citizens of a democracy expect their armed forces to be skilled warriors, capable of deterring and defeating threats to their national interest; they hold military members to a high standard of professional and personal integrity, higher than other government officials, appointed or elected. In a democracy, the role of the armed forces is defined by laws enforceable by courts of law, established by national cultural attitudes of the people, and enshrined in the ethos of the armed forces themselves. While the specifics vary from country to country, the mature democracies have evolved a set of authorities, procedures, and practices that ensure that the armed forces play a positive role, are not involved in political activity, and are directed and overseen by other organizations of the government as well as observed closely by nongovernmental institutions such as a free press (see box on p. 17). In summary, the armed forces are a competent, honest, and respected defender of the nation's interest, loyal and responsive to the elected national government.

Constitutional and Legal Foundation

In democracies the roles and functions of the armed forces are established in constitutional and legal frameworks. These legal frameworks specify the authority of the head of state to give orders to the armed forces, the authority and responsibilities of other officials in the government such as ministers of defense and their staffs, and the role of legislative bodies. They set out the procedures for sending units of the armed forces into combat, appointing and approving senior officers, providing military budgets, and purchasing military equipment and supplies.

Importantly, they provide the basis for legal orders to the armed forces. In 2003, for example, Admiral Michael Boyce, the chief of the British defense staff and senior uniformed officer in the armed forces, requested a legal opinion from the attorney general regarding the legality of the prime minister's order to invade Iraq. British troops were poised for combat, but the United Nations had not given approval for military action, and there was strong and public controversy in the United Kingdom concerning both the wisdom and legality of the invasion. Admiral Boyce considered it essential to establish that the orders to his forces were legal.

The responsibilities of the legislature of a country for its armed forces are especially important in a democracy. Although the government directs the armed forces on a day-to-day basis, and the head of government is generally the commander-in-chief of the armed forces, in a democracy the legislature has vital responsibilities. It is the legislature that approves the budget of the armed forces and, in most democracies, approves the appointments of the most senior officers; the legislature also

Seven Characteristics of Armed Forces in a Democracy

➤ Established in the constitution and legal code of the country.

➤ Assigned the primary mission of external defense, with domestic missions conducted under strict legal controls.

➤ Representative of the ethnic, regional, religious, and tribal makeup of the country, and expected to contribute to society after military service.

➤ Politically neutral, aligned with no political party.

➤ Supervised by a competent ministry of defense.

➤ Supported by a national budget, providing adequate compensation and administered without corruption.

➤ Respected by the citizenry and promoted on merit.

approves a government decision to go to war and has oversight responsibility for the armed forces, to investigate mistakes and failures and hold the government accountable for them. Legislatures in mature democracies develop experience and expertise in military matters to provide effective oversight; they exert an important constraint on executive power.

In the transitions from military regimes to democratic governments, the process of creating and promulgating the new legal framework for the armed forces is vital and often difficult. In Spain the process took a decade. Although General Francisco Franco died in 1975, it was not until 1984 that the law passed that established the authority of the minister of defense over the council of the service chiefs.[4] In South Africa a decade was spent integrating the former defense forces of the apartheid regime with the guerrilla units that had been fighting them. In Chile General Augusto Pinochet left office in 1988, but the code of military justice, dating from 1944, is currently in the process of revision.[5]

Mission

In democracies armed forces have the primary mission of defense against external threats. External threats include both immediate military threats within the region and more distant threats to the international order that have provoked a response from the United Nations. Some democracies have the good fortune not to be under direct threat from their neighbors. Other than the United States, New Zealand and Chile are also examples. For these countries, the primary mission of the armed forces is to maintain sovereignty over land, air, and maritime territory, a minimum capability that can be expanded should future threats arise, and to support international peacekeeping operations against common threats to the international community.

The armed forces of democracies are often used for operations within their countries' borders. The purpose of these operations ranges from prolonged national development missions, such as bridge and road building in Senegal, to disaster relief operations, like those of the Japanese Self-Defense Forces following the earthquake, tsunami, and Fukushima reactor disaster in 2011, to counterinsurgency or counternarcotics operations, such as those in India or Mexico, or the support of law enforcement by the British armed forces in Northern Ireland.

In democracies, internal operations are always under strict legal controls, especially regarding the use of force and handling of detained citizens. They are conducted to the extent possible in support of domestic government agencies, including domestic law enforcement agencies, and are conducted for limited periods, subject to renewal by established government procedures. Military intelligence agencies in democracies are permitted to gather information about a country's citizens only under strict controls that are approved outside the intelligence services themselves and through legal procedures.

U.S. Marines and Pakistani soldiers unload supplies during humanitarian relief operations in response to heavy flooding in Khyber Pakhtunkhwa, Pakistan, in 2010. (U.S. Marine Corps photo by Capt. Paul Duncan/Released)

The cases of the Philippines and Indonesia are both examples of the dangers of the armed forces becoming too deeply involved in dealing with internal security threats. In operations against two insurgencies, the Armed Forces of the Philippines under the autocratic regime of President Ferdinand Marcos were actually given formal authority over the police.[6] In addition, military officers were given national development responsibilities such as education and health. The corruption and incompetence the officers observed, along with their direct involvement in nonmilitary matters, encouraged them to take direct action to change government through coups. For many years Indonesian military officers were assigned to civilian government positions, from the legislature to district government posts, leaving many of them with little respect for the authority of elected government officials.[7] Part of the maturing process of Philippine and Indonesian democracy in recent years has been the withdrawal of the armed forces from these domestic roles.

Contribution to Society

There are procedures established within the armed forces of democracies to ensure that they reflect the ethnic, regional, religious, and tribal makeup of their country. In the United States, for example, there are specific programs to encourage the recruitment and promotion of officers from ethnic minorities; in Senegal there are laws to ensure that all religious and ethnic groups have access to military service. In El Salvador and South Africa, when the armed forces were reconstituted following civil war, both guerillas and government soldiers who had fought each other for years were included in the armed forces established after the war. This mixing of groups in the armed forces is intended not only to provide service opportunities for different segments of the society but also to ensure that the armed forces retain a national perspective, not favoring one group within the country because of their composition.[8] Integration of minority groups within the armed forces has been most successful when it has been carried down to the unit level. When entire brigades have been of a single ethnic group, they have been susceptible to appeals for secession or coup. The Nigerian civil war of the 1960s provided a prime example of this danger.

In democracies, when veterans of military service return to civilian life, they are expected to contribute to a country's overall objectives through the skills and knowledge they gained during their service. In several democracies, such as Singapore, the Republic of Korea, Taiwan, and Israel, there is universal service. All citizens around the age of twenty serve for a period of time in the armed forces. These countries expect that the time their young men and women spend in uniform will build a sense of patriotism as well as instill the values of discipline and teamwork. When they return to civilian life, these veterans contribute to society at a higher level of performance. In Israel, for example, successful entrepreneurs often attribute much of their success to the skills they learned during their military service. In developing democratic countries, soldiers, sailors, and airmen returning to civilian life are generally more patriotic, better educated, and more technically skilled than those who have not served and thus can make a greater contribution to the development of their countries.

> *Armed forces in a democracy are competent, honest, and respected defenders of the nation's interest, loyal and responsive to the elected national government.*

Political Neutrality

In democracies, the armed forces are expected to be just as loyal and responsive to the orders of a new government on its first day in office as they were to the previous government on its last day. Active duty military personnel play no role in elections beyond casting their individual votes, and they do not make any political preference known publicly. During political crises, they remain neutral.

It is not always easy to apply these simple guidelines to the many complex situations that arise in the political life of either established democracies or transitional democracies that have recently been ruled by autocratic regimes. In established democracies, senior military officers are expected to take positions on issues that are important to military effectiveness. For example, in the United States, the issue of allowing homosexuals to serve in the armed forces has been controversial for many years. Chairman of the Joint Chiefs of Staff General Colin Powell took the public position in 1992 that it would be detrimental to military effectiveness for homosexuals to serve openly, whereas by 2009 his successor Admiral Mike Mullen took the position that it would be favorable. When a government decides to reduce military budgets, military leaders are expected to state publicly the effect of the reductions on military capability, but they are to do so in a way that does not align their statements with a political party. If a military leader in a democracy feels that he cannot support the policies of the government, it is his responsibility to resign, as did General Ronald Fogleman, chief of staff of the Air Force, when the Clinton administration in the mid-1990s was reducing his service's budget to what he considered a dangerous point.

In countries that do not have the advantage of long-established democracies, political crises will often place senior military leaders in very difficult positions. Civilian political leaders who are challenging the current government will attempt to gain their support by promising privilege and favors. Such was the case in the past with the Colorado Party in Paraguay and the Kuomintang (Chinese Nationalist Party) in Taiwan. Military leaders in these countries have been able to resist these attempts in recent years. More commonly, current political leaders will attempt to use the armed forces to maintain or increase their own power in ways that are clearly inconsistent with democratic principles. After Thaksin Shinawatra won election as president of Thailand, he made assignments and promotions in the Thai armed forces with the clear objective of placing his supporters in important military leadership positions. Although as president he had the authority to approve senior officer appointments, his actions were part of an overall strategy to gain personal control of the Thai government and rule in an autocratic manner. However, the Thai military leadership ultimately deposed President Thaksin.[9] In the Philippines in 2001, President Joseph Estrada ordered Chief of Defense Angelo Reyes to send soldiers out to Edsa Square to end the protests against the Estrada government. Although the directive from the president was justified on the grounds of restoring civil order, General Angelo Reyes knew that his actions would be decisive in whether the Estrada government stayed in office or would resign. He decided to refer the president's order to the Philippine supreme court for a ruling on its legality. His action was widely interpreted as a lack of support for the president, who soon resigned. In both these cases, military leaders acted to thwart an elected president acting in an undemocratic manner. The coup by the Thai armed forces countered one undemocratic action with another, whereas General Reyes' decision to refer to the supreme court achieved the objective of checking an undemocratic leader without a coup.

There are rarely simple, correct answers in situations like the ones described above. Military leaders must think through the issues at stake carefully and make decisions based on supporting the long-term democratic development of their counties. History generally judges favorably those generals and admirals who do so, and since honor and legacy are important to most senior officers, they often make the correct and courageous decision.

Ministries of Defense

In democracies military leaders provide advice on military policies, but the ultimate decisions on the structure and funding of the armed forces and on their employment rest with the elected government. Ministries of defense perform the function of receiving professional military advice from the uniformed services and then implementing the national decisions that affect the armed forces. There is an appointed or confirmed minister of defense with a staff that has the authority and skills for these responsibilities. The minister of defense is responsible both to the head of government and to the legislature for the approval of defense policy, the appointment of senior military officers, the approval of defense budgets and major equipment purchases, and the overall direction of military operations. Although military officers can serve in assignments within the ministry of defense, the top positions in democracies are all civilian politicians or senior career government employees. A strong and competent ministry of defense ensures that the military leaders of the armed forces are not making their own policy decisions, and in addition it insulates them from political deal making. Both functions are important to the armed forces in a democracy.

Developing competent ministries of defense staffed by skilled civilian personnel in countries in which they have never existed is one of the more difficult challenges facing a country transitioning to democracy. Under military regimes, uniformed officers in the military services have been performing all the staff functions—policymaking, planning, personnel management, communications, procurement, budgeting—and there are simply no civilians with the required technical skills. Most countries making the transition assemble staff for their newly created ministries of defense with a combination of officials seconded from other departments of government and experienced military officers on loan or recently retired. The Eastern European countries that had been part of the Soviet Union–dominated Warsaw Pact did not have competent national ministries of defense. When they gained their independence after the cold war ended, many of them aspired to NATO membership, and they struggled with the challenges of developing their defense ministry staffs. In Hungary, for example, the training of civil servants in the ministry of defense and the education of newly elected members of the legislature with no military experience was one of the key challenges for the NATO military assistance missions of the 1990s.[10] Unless a country undertakes a training and education program to develop a competent cadre of defense civil servants, and unless political leaders both in the government and in the legislature develop an interest and expertise in defense matters, then there will not be a strong ministry of defense performing the all-important function of linking the military services to political direction and control.

Budgets, Pay, and Procurement

Military budgets are big. Within a country they can account for 1 to10 percent of the entire gross domestic product. With access to large funds come large incentives for control and corruption. The established democracies have developed systems to ensure that their armed forces are adequately funded for their missions and that the funds are spent on the intended purposes and not siphoned off into the pockets of the powerful.

In mature democracies, military budgets are funded entirely by the national government as approved by the legislature. Military units do not have their own businesses generating profits to pay salaries and expenses nor farms to raise their own food; they do not issue telecommunications licenses and apply the fees to their own purposes. Military budgets are published so that citizens know how much their government is spending on defense and where the budget is going. The systems to purchase supplies and equipment are transparent. The competitive procedures, costs, and responsibilities of all officials involved are established by law, audited, and published. Legislatures have the staff, authority, and responsibility to track closely the expenditure of defense funds to ensure that they are being used for their intended purposes.

Military personnel of all ranks are paid adequately in the armed forces of mature democracies through salary, housing, medical care, and pension so that there is neither incentive nor necessity to take bribes or extort payments.

Prestige, Reputation, Rights, and Opportunity

In the established democracies, the armed forces routinely rank in opinion polls as one of the most respected institutions in the country. They are considered defenders of their country who

are willing to serve, despite personal hardship and the obligation to give their lives for their country, out of patriotism and
a higher sense of service. In Chile today, a little over twenty
years since General Pinochet left office, military officers have
the highest respect of any profession in the country. In the
United States today, military personnel traveling in uniform are
invited to board airplanes ahead of first class passengers. In all
democracies, to have served in the armed forces is considered
a substantial advantage to a politician in an election. Military
participants are a part of national celebrations, displaying the
flag and providing honor guards for the burial of distinguished

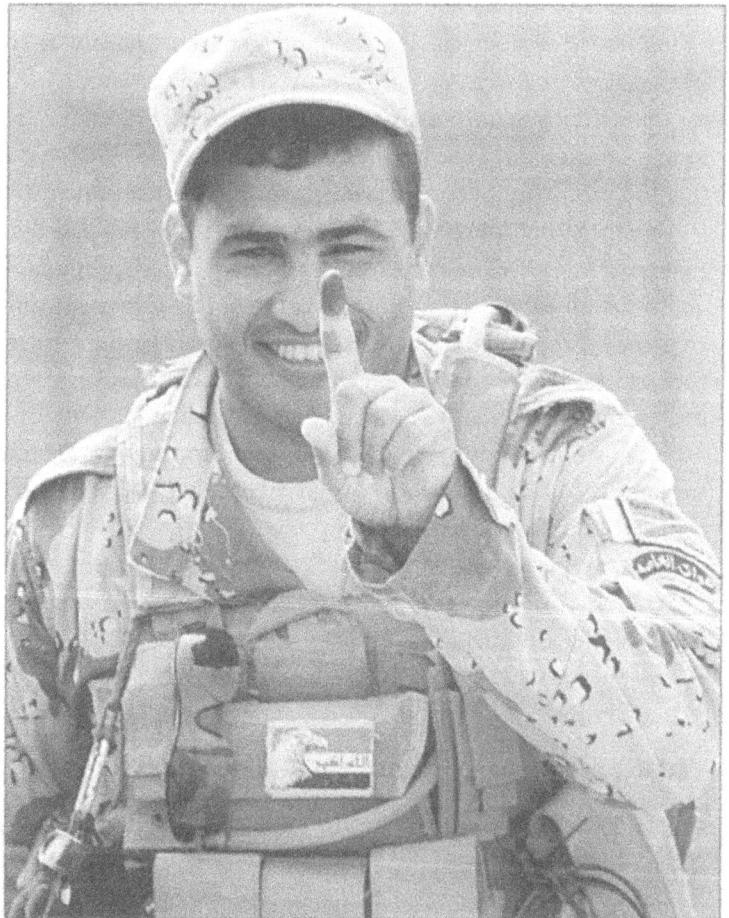

An Iraqi solider shows
that he has voted.

national leaders. When they are committed to action, popular support grows, especially when they suffer casualties. Even when wars lose popular support, the citizens of democracies understand that the armed forces who fight those wars are performing honorable duties, and citizens continue to support them and honor the sacrifices they make in their countries' service. In Israel hundreds of prisoners will be exchanged for a single Israeli soldier.

Members of the armed forces in democracies do not have all the personal freedoms of the other citizens in their countries. They give up some of their rights to free speech and political activity, and much of their right to privacy. In return, they are owed fair treatment within the military system through promotion based on merit, adequate compensation, and a military justice system that protects the rights of the accused as it pursues just verdicts and supports military discipline.

The promotion system based on merit is especially important in the armed forces of democracies. Often the opportunities for advancement within the service are much greater than they are in the country as a whole. This has been true in the United States, for example, in the case of African Americans. They were allowed to serve freely in the U.S. military after World War II and for many years advanced much further within the armed forces than they could in civilian life, where they were restricted by laws and prejudice. In democratic countries with social stratification, such as the United Kingdom, the armed forces have always offered those from less privileged backgrounds the opportunity to advance based on their intelligence, skill, and persistence.

Conclusion

This chapter has presented seven aspects of the armed forces in established democracies that distinguish them from those in autocratic regimes. These have evolved in many countries over the years and have resulted in an arrangement that is of mutual benefit to the members of the armed forces themselves and to the government and people of the country they serve. The members of the armed forces receive great respect from their fellow citizens, consistent and adequate pay, and the opportunity to advance by their merits; in return, the democratic nations gain capable warriors who will use their power not to threaten the elected government but to defend their fellow citizens under the government's lawful orders.

3

Regional Transitions
to Democracy

Political scientists write of three waves of global democratization, with the Arab Awakening possibly constituting the start of a fourth. The first wave, which began in the early nineteenth century, crested and retreated with only twelve democracies remaining in 1942.

The second wave began at the end of World War II and crested in 1962 with thirty-six established democracies in the world. Many of these new democracies were former European colonies in Asia and Africa. By the early 1970s, however, several had fallen back into dictatorship.

The third wave of democratic development began in the mid-1970s, and was the most powerful (see table 3-1). In Western Europe, Spain, Portugal, and Greece moved from military-supported dictatorships to democracies; when the Soviet Union collapsed, roughly twelve counties in Central and Eastern Europe became democratic. In Latin America, nine countries made the transition, and in Asia six military-supported dictatorships became democracies. Several African countries maintained democratic systems, although total numbers did not increase. As of this writing, the total number of democracies in the world has passed 100.

A fourth wave began with the Arab Awakening in January 2011. Although transitions are still in process throughout the region, it is likely that Tunisia and several other countries in the Middle East and North Africa will become solid democracies.

Just as remarkable as the sheer numbers of countries that have become democracies is their geographical, cultural, and ethnic diversity. The desire to choose one's own form of government and to enjoy basic freedoms and rights is not limited to a region, race, or religion; it is a universal human aspiration.

Although there are marked differences in the paths of democratic development among the major geopolitical regions of the world, there are also similarities. There are strong interactions among the countries within each of five major world regions—Europe and Central Asia, Latin America, East and South Asia, Africa, and the Middle East and North Africa. Volume 2 of this handbook presents detailed accounts of the military role in democratic development for each of the regions and the role outside influences played. In addition, there are fourteen case histories of individual countries within the regions. This chapter presents a brief overview of democratic transitions within the five major regions.

Europe and Central Asia

Most countries of Western Europe have had long-established democracies, well-defined roles for their armed forces, and solid civil-military relations.[1] This prevailing practice in the region strongly influenced the smaller number of European countries

TABLE 3-1. Third-Wave Transitions to Democracy, 1974–92

Region	Number of countries
Africa	0
Asia	6
Central and Eastern Europe	12
Latin America	9
Western Europe	3

with autocratic regimes. Transitions to democracy in these countries followed different paths. West Germany's democratic structure was imposed by the victorious and democratic United States, United Kingdom, and France following World War II and has endured and even strengthened since the departure of occupation forces. When the cold war ended and East Germans joined their countrymen in the West, they learned democratic practices quickly. An East German–educated politician is now Germany's chancellor. France's unique democratic system withstood an unsuccessful coup by disgruntled military officers at the end of the Algerian independence war. In Greece a military coup in the 1960s was justified by the threat of a communist takeover by election; within seven years, the Greek junta collapsed due to internal conflict, popular opposition, and heavy external pressure. Spain and Portugal were ruled by dictators with military support from the 1920s until the 1970s, when both made peaceful transitions to democracy. In Spain's case, the desire to join NATO was a strong incentive to reform. Today, military involvement in political issues has become almost unthinkable in Western Europe.

During the cold war years, Central and Eastern European countries were governed by autocratic communist regimes in turn dominated by the Soviet Union. In most of the East European countries, armed forces did not play a significant role in the transitions to democracy. From its founding, the Russian Communist Party never trusted the country's armed forces and instituted stringent procedures to ensure that they were controlled by the party. These procedures were replicated in the Warsaw Pact states throughout the cold war, and in addition Soviet military officers held command positions in the armed forces of other Warsaw Pact states. When the Soviet Union collapsed, most of the newly autonomous countries established democratic governments and sought to join NATO, in large measure to protect themselves from a potentially resurgent future Russia. Under its Membership Action Plan, NATO established criteria for entry that incorporated most of the aspects of armed forces in a democracy that are described in the preceding chapter. By satisfying the NATO requirements, Bulgaria, the Czech Republic, Estonia, Hungary, Latvia, Lithuania, Poland, Romania, and Slovakia all became members, as did Croatia and Slovenia after the breakup of Yugoslavia, with its wars in Bosnia and Kosovo. In a number of the transitioning East European states, the armed forces struggled during the democratization process, with the old guard of more senior officers being less supportive and the younger junior and midgrade officers being more willing to embrace change. The support from NATO members for alliance membership served as a strong catalytic influence toward democracy during this process. Several member states of the former Soviet Union, notably Belarus (and many of the Central Asian countries), have subsequently reverted to autocratic regimes led by former communist officials, while others, such as Ukraine and even Hungary, have lost democratic ground.[2]

In the Central Asian countries of the former Soviet Union, communist officials generally were able to remain in power by winning elections and then consolidating control over the newly formed governments. Only in Kyrgyzstan have democratic processes shown any life. The armed forces in Central Asian countries have been passive during the political events following independence. Central Asian states like Kazakhstan work very hard to maintain a balance of influence among Russia, China, and the West. The strongest immediate influences on their armed forces come from Russia and China, neither of which favors democratic development. However, none of these countries is completely closed, and the influence of democratic ideas and the example of the Arab Awakening, along with routine contact with democratic countries and international organizations, ensure that the potential for democratic transition is present.

Latin America

Over the course of the last half century, Latin America has moved from a region of widespread dictatorship to one in which democracy prevails, with the armed forces playing a central role

in each transition.[3] The countries of the region had all won
their independence through armed revolutions during the nineteenth century, and military leaders and armies had been deeply
involved in political development since liberation. By the late
1970s, military dictators were in power in Argentina, Bolivia,
Brazil, Chile, Ecuador, El Salvador, Honduras, Paraguay, and
Peru. From 1978, when the military regime in Ecuador began
a transition to democracy, through 1992, when the civil war in
El Salvador ended through a UN-sponsored peace process and
elections were held, all nine of these countries made transitions
to democracy.

The process within each country was unique, but there were
common features. In virtually every case, divisions within the
military-supported dictatorships loosened regime cohesion and
opened the way to democratic development. Popular pressure
for democracy was always a factor, as authoritarian regimes
generally could not sustain economic prosperity (Chile was
an exception) and resorted to repressive measures to maintain order. As they relinquished power, military governments
sought, with varying degrees of success, to negotiate institutional assurances and privileges under subsequent governments.
These included amnesty for actions during military rule, guar-
anteed budget allocations, and limited external oversight. The
Argentine junta, for example, having mismanaged the economy
and lost a war to the United Kingdom, had no standing when it
was driven from power in 1982. The leaders of the junta were
prosecuted, and military budgets were cut drastically. In Brazil
a military government began to turn over power to an elected
government in 1982 while keeping its reputation intact. The
Brazilian military adjusted easily to a subordinate role and was
funded adequately for its traditional regional activities. In other
cases, including Chile, Honduras, and Paraguay, it took years
after the military's departure from power to establish solid civil-
military relations.[4]

In these Latin American democratic transitions, internal
forces and dynamics were the driving factors. However, external influences, primarily from the United States, played both

negative and positive roles. During the cold war, when Cuba and the Soviet Union were often supporting revolutions against authoritarian governments, American anticommunism often trumped pro-democratic policies. American military training, although it included instruction on subjects like rules of engagement and respect for noncombatants, emphasized military counterinsurgency operations. However, with the end of the cold war, U.S. military relations with Latin American counterparts emphasized democratic development. Other outside influences included the Catholic Church. Although the Church's official position was not consistently against autocratic governments, individual priests sometimes moderated the repressive actions of military units, and the Vatican facilitated the transition in El Salvador, for example. Other Latin American countries also made a difference—Mexico played a key role in the negotiations

Brazilian peacekeepers in Haiti. (Photo by MATEUS_27:24&25/Flickr)

between the Salvadoran government and the Farabundo Martí National Liberation Front.

East and South Asia

Beginning in the 1950s, there was a surge of military governments and military-backed regimes in Asia, increasing from one (Thailand) in 1950 to nine in the early 1980s.[5] All Asian nations except Japan are relatively new states; most achieved independent statehood in the aftermath of World War II. Protomilitary forces played crucial roles in the construction and protection of new states from internal and external threats after liberating their countries from colonial rule or fighting revolutionary wars. Lacking confidence in feuding civilian political leaders and in budding democratic institutions, many militaries saw themselves as the only reliable guardians of their states. Perceiving strong governance as crucial for state security and economic development, militaries often allied with authoritarian and autocratic governments, or they themselves assumed the mantle of government. During the cold war, the international environment was also supportive of authoritarian and autocratic governments that were anticommunist. The high level of concern with state security and economic development often gave the military pride of place. The military then used its privileged position to strengthen the power and influence of military leaders and institutions, enabling them to expand their role and limit democratic political development. A vicious cycle was set in motion.

Even under these conditions, democratic institutions developed in many Asian countries and became stronger over the years. During the 1980s and 1990s, the armed forces of the Republic of Korea and Taiwan shifted their support from ruling parties to elected governments. Since the 1986 People Power Revolution in the Philippines, there has been a steady trend in the direction of democratic civil-military relations, albeit with setbacks, for example, in Thailand and Sri Lanka. In Indonesia the armed forces, carefully cultivated by an authoritarian ruler for decades, withdrew their support for the regime when popular opposition arose.[6]

Military and military-backed governments in Asia (and elsewhere) often staked their legitimacy on the promise of security, stability, economic development, and international support. Success, as well as failure, in delivering these promises, along with change in the international environment, broke the vicious cycle established earlier. Economic growth did initially bolster the legitimacy of authoritarian and autocratic governments. Over time, however, sustained economic development strengthened the capacity of other state institutions, broadened the base of middle and working classes, and made for a much more complex society. Growing civil and political societies resisted authoritarian and autocratic rule and demanded greater political participation and government accountability. Income inequality concerns arising from unequal distribution of the benefits of rapid economic growth, or in some cases from economic crisis and failure, undermined the legitimacy of military-backed authoritarian governments. At the same time, traditional state security concerns lessened for many countries. Over time the international environment too became less supportive of authoritarian and autocratic rule. With the disintegration of the Soviet Union, the communist model became less credible, and Soviet support for socialist and nondemocratic states collapsed. Emphasizing human rights, democracy, and markets, the United States became less supportive of authoritarian and autocratic regimes.

The combination of these events undermined the rationale for military or military-backed rule as a way to stabilize and develop the country, as well as the privileged position of the military within the state. Sensing the changing and complex nature of economics and society and the shifting balance of power within and among state institutions, political society, and civil society, as well as the growing domestic and international democratic trends (including the increased support for pro-democratic civil societies), some militaries began to redefine their places in society and roles in the state. Positioning themselves for the postauthoritarian era to protect their institutional and personal interests and seeking to avoid bloodshed and further tarnish the image of the military, some military leaders in crucial positions withdrew support for authoritarian and autocratic rulers or refrained from obstructing democratic transitions. In a few cases, military leaders with democratic inclinations facilitated such transitions.

Countries that developed strong democratic institutions, processes, and practices utilized civilian expertise on matters of defense and security during their transitions. The balance of power shifted, and the military was compelled to accept and abide by democratic civilian control. The practice and enforcement of democratic civilian control became a core belief of the military, political, and civil societies over time. Failure to develop strong democratic institutions and practices, along with inadequate expertise, resources, capacity, and competence on the part of civilian leaders and institutions, allowed the military to continue its direct or indirect involvement in politics in some countries, such as Pakistan and Bangladesh. Protection of institutional and personal interests also explains continued military involvement in politics and the slow pace of or setbacks in democratic civilian control of the military in these countries.

At the time of this writing, North Korea, Myanmar (which is in the initial phase of transition), and China remain autocratic countries supported by their armed forces, and in Pakistan the government remains in power only with the permission of the armed forces.

Africa

The countries of sub-Saharan Africa achieved their independence and self-governance through various methods.[7] In 1957 Ghana became the first former colony to be granted independence; South Africa did not achieve majority rule until 1994. Most of these independent African countries became one-party states, with revolutionary leaders replacing colonial masters. Through the 1980s, only five of the forty-seven sub-Saharan African countries were democracies.

The armed forces of newly independent countries in which there was a peaceful transfer of power—Ghana, Senegal, and others—were generally formed on the basis of the colonial security forces. For those countries that had defeated white minority rulers in liberation wars—Angola, Zimbabwe, and South Africa—the armed forces were formed from the military wings of the freedom parties. For those countries that fought civil wars following independence—Angola, Rwanda, and the Democratic Republic of the Congo, among others—overcoming the brutal legacy of internal conflict has made formation of national armed forces even more difficult.

Following the end of the cold war in 1989, there was spate of multiparty elections in Africa—thirty-seven of them—but little democracy. The armed forces of most countries either assisted dictators in rigging elections in order to remain in power or overturned election results, as was the case in twelve countries that underwent military coups.

With a few notable exceptions, such as Senegal and South Africa, the armed forces in most African countries are becoming more involved in internal political affairs. Individual officers understand the theory of the role of the armed forces in a democracy, but the immaturity of other state institutions, lack of economic development, and tribal loyalties all create pressure on military leaders and units to join internal power struggles. The Mali coup in March 2012, which senior Mali military leaders condemned but were unable to overcome, was illustrative of this trend.

Outside countries and organizations are involved in security sector reform programs throughout the region and are working to improve various aspects of civil-military relations. In addition, African organizations such as the West African Union and the Organization of African Unity are becoming bolder in condemning antidemocratic trends and actions within member countries. However, democratic institutions and civil-military relations are underdeveloped in sub-Saharan African countries, and it will require additional years of effort to achieve solid democratic forms of government.

The Middle East and North Africa

The countries of this region gained their independence from colonial rule as early as 1920 (Turkey) and as late as 1961 (Kuwait).[8] Through the period of the cold war, the armed forces of the newly independent countries were shaped by their colonial heritage, the ethnic and tribal nature of their populations, and their cold war sponsors, either the United States and other NATO states or the Soviet Union. Democracies were few in number—Israel and, for a time, Lebanon. In Turkey the armed forces maintained a privileged position, intervening periodically

During the Arab Awakening, a crowd gathers in Amman, Jordan, after Friday prayers. (Photo by Charles Fred/Flickr)

in the government, but gradually elected governments asserted control and reduced their independence and power. Autocratic regimes ruled the rest of the region, some of them coming to power in military coups and all supported by their military forces. There seemed to be little chance for democratic development in the region. The dictators, many of them former military men with Soviet sponsorship and Chinese assistance, faced no pressure to reform. U.S. advocacy of democracy in the region was muted by cold war imperatives and its dependence on oil from the region, and undercut by its support for Israel. The end of the cold war in 1989 brought hope for democratic development: Soviet influence and assistance withered, the United States adopted the promotion of democracy as a policy objective, and a broad-based coalition of forces led by the United States pushed Iraqi troops out of Kuwait. For the next twenty years, although no new democracies emerged, forces for change were gathering beneath the surface. They flashed and were quenched in Lebanon in 2005 and Iran in 2009, and then erupted again in 2011 when peaceful protests challenged long-established dictators throughout the region. The armed forces continued to support autocratic governments in Bahrain and Syria. However, in Tunisia, Egypt, Libya, and Yemen, military leaders turned on their former commanders and forced them from power. At the time of this writing, the outcomes of the transitions in these countries are uncertain, but autocrats in the region are on notice that they cannot count on their military forces to suppress the aspirations of their people for dignity and representative government.

Conclusion

Across five major regions of the world, armed forces have participated in four waves of democratic transition. Each country's story has been unique, but some common features have emerged. Special circumstances, including exceptional leadership, have allowed some countries to start the transition well in advance of others in their region; Turkey and South Africa are major examples. In other regions, a combination of political and economic circumstances led to clusters of transitions: economic mismanagement by autocratic regimes and the end of left-wing insurgencies in Latin America, the breakup of the Warsaw Pact in Europe, prosperity and the strengthening of political structures in Asia, and economic failure and corruption in the Middle East and North Africa. To date only in Africa and Central Asia have stable democratic governments failed to establish themselves widely. While armed forces have rarely been in the vanguard of democratic change, today there is no military dictatorship in the world (with the possible exception of tiny Fiji), and military leaders everywhere generally acknowledge the superiority of representative government, although they argue that their countries may not be ready for democracy yet, and they try to preserve as much autonomy and privileges for their services as they can. Outside influences have sometimes helped to delay transitions, but the trend is that the governments, multilateral organizations, and nongovernmental groups of the established democracies increasingly use their influence to help bring other countries out of dictatorship. In the future, the armed forces of the increasing number of established democracies have great opportunities to continue and reinforce the democratizing trends of the past.

4

Developing Democracy: The Crucial Role of the Armed Forces

Military forces have played decisive roles in most major political changes in countries worldwide. Many countries won their independence through armed struggle, civil wars have determined the course of a country's history, and international wars resulted in the gain or loss of territory and the preservation or loss of sovereignty. Although the fighting ended, military leaders and the units they commanded continued to wield power in political life.

There have been exceptions. Some countries achieved significant political transformations without the use of military force: India won its independence from Great Britain without war, South Africa ended apartheid without a civil war, and Singapore left the Federation of Malaysia without a fight. Sometimes after a conflict ends, a country is fortunate enough to have military leaders who followed the example of the Roman hero Cincinnatus, twice dictator of his country and twice returned to his farm. George Washington and Kemal Atatürk are other prominent examples.

However, it is more often the case that when military force has been the critical factor in political development, military leaders and their troops develop a sense of responsibility for their countries' further political development and a sense of entitlement to intervene in politics when dissatisfied with the course of later events.

Armed forces around the world have a history of political involvement. Military intervention was commonplace for many years in Latin America, a region in which all countries gained their independence through armed struggles during the nineteenth century. In East Asia, the same was true for Indonesia when it gained its independence in 1947. Although the armed forces of South Korea and Taiwan could not take credit for the independence of their countries, they used their civil war credentials to exercise authoritarian power. The armed forces of Thailand and Pakistan have assumed the same entitlement, without having earned it by any feat of arms. In the Middle East and North Africa, the Turkish armed forces, contrary to the example of Kemal Atatürk, awarded themselves guardianship of their country's government for their role in the Turkish War of Independence.[1] The armed forces of Algeria have continued to intervene in politics when they judge the country to have gone astray. Armies in Egypt, Iraq, and Syria quickly assumed a sense of both responsibility and entitlement stemming less from their martial achievements than from their status as the most respected and competent organizations in otherwise underdeveloped countries and from their armed and disciplined power. Sub-Saharan Africa has experienced a mix of armed liberation struggles and independence granted by colonial masters. However, in each case, the armies were involved in politics from the beginning and have continued to intervene frequently. At the time of this writing, military units in Mali have defied the government in the northern part of the country.

Only in the United States, Canada, and Europe have the armed forces stayed out of the internal political life of their countries. In Western Europe, mature democratic systems have established a respected, professional external defense role for their armed forces; decades of tight, often ruthless, government control based on the Russian Leninist model have generally deterred the armed forces of Eastern Europe and Central Asia from coups. Even within this overall pattern, there have been isolated military influences and interventions: the Spanish Army's strong role in the Franco government, the Greek coup in 1967, and the half-hearted military participation in the attempted coup against Russian President Mikhail Gorbachev in 1991.

Uneasy Alliances: Dictators and Their Armed Forces

Pure military dictatorships, with generals running all the functions of government and martial law in effect, are relatively rare. Now that Myanmar has made a dramatic shift toward reform, Fiji, hardly a global trendsetter, is the world's only true military dictatorship. The military took power in a coup in 2006, and the current prime minister, Commodore Josaia Bainimarama, is the commander of Fiji's armed forces. In most cases, military leaders have found that their officers and troops do not have the full range of skills to maintain a successful civil administration, and the armed forces lose their coherence as a separate organization. In addition, especially when things go badly for a country's economy, popular resentment, without the safety valve of democratic elections, places great pressure on authoritarian governments. Military leaders who lead coups soon find that most government functions are best done by others.

One-party dictatorships supported by the armed forces are more common than pure military dictatorships. In these cases, a strong leader (often an ex-military officer) and his party have taken over a government and have maintained the support of the armed forces through a combination of rewards and ruthlessness. In Paraguay the armed forces were intertwined with the Colorado Party from the beginning of President Alfredo Stroessner's rule in 1954. In South Korea, the army supported the Liberal Party and later the Democratic Republican Party, and in Taiwan the armed forces partnered with the Kuomintang to maintain a dictatorship for several decades. In the Middle East, the Iraqi and Syrian armies supported the Baathist Party. In North Africa, Algerian President Abdelaziz Bouteflika depends on the support of the Algerian army. Likewise, Colonel Muammar Qaddafi, who overthrew the Libyan monarchy in a coup in 1969, used military support to stay in power until 2011. In Zimbabwe Robert Mugabe and the Zimbabwe African National Union–Patriotic Front have maintained the control and support of the Zimbabwe Defense Forces.

An alliance between the dictator and armed forces can take a variety of forms. In such an alliance, both sides attempt to gain advantages and minimize vulnerabilities. For the dictator, the primary advantage is the personal loyalty of the armed forces, and he will use both rewards and punishment to achieve and maintain it. For example, President Ferdinand Marcos of the Philippines notoriously presented each of his generals with an expensive watch to win their loyalty. Dictators allow generals

The vice president of The Gambia, Dr. Isatou Njie-Saidy, arrives aboard a U.S. Navy ship in 2012. The Gambia is not yet an established democracy. (U.S. Navy photo by Mass Communication Specialist 2nd Class Josh Bennett/Released)

to profit from the corruption that is endemic to most autocratic societies. A dictator's most powerful weapon is the control of military leadership positions, and he promotes those he considers loyal and discharges or prosecutes those whose loyalty is suspect. Dictators value loyalty far more than military skill, and their armed forces are most often led by trustworthy, wealthy incompetents. Military leaders who become too competent, even in war, are feared rather than thanked by their dictators, who see them as potential competitors. Marshal Georgy Zhukov, the most capable and successful Soviet general of the Second World War, was fired by Stalin within a year of the Allied victory. North Korean dictators Kim Il Sung and Kim Jong Il showered public praise and scarce resources on the armed forces but rotated army commanders to prevent any individuals from becoming too established and powerful. In Libya Muammar Qaddafi never established a potentially powerful commander of his army but ordered individual unit commanders to report directly to him.

Dictators also use other branches of government either to keep a balance of power within the military services or to keep tabs on their loyalty. In Saudi Arabia, the armed forces and the national guard have comparable capabilities and separate chains of command; in Iran the Islamic Revolutionary Guard Corps duplicates the capability of the regular Iranian armed forces. In most countries with a communist legacy, such as China, ruling party commissars serve as political assistants to military commanders and report privately on their political reliability. In many dictatorships, the intelligence services report separately to the dictator not only on opposition movements but also on the actions of the regular armed forces.

For their part, the armed forces in dictatorships attempt to ensure a reliable flow of financial and human resources and the preservation of their institutional independence. Resources come both from government revenues and businesses controlled by the armed forces. Some receive lucrative fees from radio and television licenses. Since 2009 the Indonesian government has been attempting to take over the military-owned businesses in industries such as logging and hotel and property development.

In Egypt the military plays a significant role in several industries including car production, food processing, property development, and construction. Militaries also run companies in other types of manufacturing, health care, and even entertainment, such as the People's Liberation Army's night clubs in China. In Iran the Islamic Revolutionary Guard Corps controls a large number of commercial companies, including many in the petrochemical sector.

In addition to their business profits, the armed forces under dictatorships are in a strong position to profit from criminal activity, including drug trafficking, shakedowns, and kickbacks. The armed forces attempt to maintain their institutional independence by blocking outside investigators, whether from the ruling party, independent intelligence services, or legislatures. The Pakistan Army has successfully resisted any oversight by the country's president, prime minister, or parliament. Before the Egyptian parliament was dissolved in June 2012, Muslim Brotherhood parliamentarians vowed to achieve civilian oversight of the military budget. However, the military rejected any attempt to examine its economic activity. As Major General Mahmoud Nasr asserted, "We will not allow anyone, whoever they may be, to come near the projects of the armed forces."[2] The Chinese People's Liberation Army is nominally accountable to civilian party leaders, but in reality party leaders have incomplete insight into its budget. Militaries insist on their personnel's subjection only to military discipline and courts, and they attempt to control promotion systems for their officers.

Political Crises in Dictatorships

The fundamental contradictions in the uneasy alliances between dictatorships and their armed forces come to the surface when the dictatorship fails to meet the economic, social, and political aspirations of the people, and the citizens call for change.

Often the leaders of the armed forces in a dictatorship recognize that the supreme ruler is losing his people's support, and they often take action to shift their own support. This was the case in Indonesia in the late 1990s, when the military leadership realized that President Suharto was losing popular support and his economic touch. Even before the dramatic events of the Arab Awakening, both the Egyptian and the Tunisian armed forces had begun to put distance between themselves and their dictators. In South Africa, it was the military intelligence services that first understood that the white regime would not be able to stay in power.

Under such circumstances, the armed forces are seldom active agents of democratic change, but they are ready for others to challenge the dictators that they are less and less willing to serve. In many cases, the opposition breaks out into public protests, strikes, or civil action of other kinds, and the dictator orders the armed forces to enforce his authority and suppress the opposition. At this point, the dictator is violating the

First Session of the Tunisian Constituent Assembly on November 22, 2011. General Rachid Ammar, on the left, had refused orders to use military force to suppress peaceful protests in Tunisia in early 2011, leading to the end of President Ben Ali's dictatorship. (Photo by Tab59/Flickr)

fundamental ethos of the armed forces, regardless of how many watches or other handouts he has given to the generals, or how carefully he has promoted loyal officers. At the heart of the military officer's creed is the solemn obligation to defend the citizens of the nation, not to shoot them. Despite this creed, the armed forces have often responded to dictators' orders and suppressed revolt. The People's Liberation Army did so in Tiananmen Square in China in 1989; through the 1990s, the Serbian army patrolled the streets of Belgrade when the police could not handle demonstrations; the Islamic Revolutionary Guard Corps arrested protesters in Iran in 2009; and, as of this writing, Syria's armed forces are supporting the Assad government with a brutal campaign against widespread opposition. However, in an increasing number of instances, military leaders have declined to prop up dictators by placing troops on the streets and have withdrawn their support. Generally the loss of military support has been the decisive factor in the fall of a dictator.

The Trends

The high watermark of military-supported dictatorships was in the early 1970s. At that time, it was difficult to be optimistic about the future of democracy in the world. Military or civilian dictatorships strongly supported by armed forces seemed the most common form of government. In Latin America, there were ten military or military-supported dictatorships; in Asia, nine; in the Middle East and North Africa, there were twenty-four; in sub-Saharan Africa, twenty-eight, and in Europe, twenty-five.

However, in the 1970s, the tide began to turn. The third wave of democratization that began at that point has been the most powerful of all, and the Arab Awakening is potentially a fourth wave. The regional summaries and case studies in volume 2 of this handbook discuss the unique characteristics of this process in different parts of the world, but there are common factors.

Economic developments played an important role in bringing down dictatorships. Sustained economic progress in many countries led to a middle class with the power, influence, and confidence to challenge authoritarian government. This effect was most pronounced in East Asia. In South Korea, Taiwan, and to a lesser extent in Thailand a newly affluent middle class formed institutions that could support democratic processes—opposition political parties, competent civil administration, justice systems, and national media. In Latin America, virtually every military and military-supported dictatorship presented itself as a temporary government that fully intended to restore electoral democracy when security and economic conditions allowed. In Brazil, Chile, and Uruguay, military governments actually kept their promises and turned power over to elected governments.

Interestingly, economic failure as well as economic success also has brought down dictatorships. Military and military-supported governments were often driven from office by poor economic performance. Economic hard times were a key factor in the Argentine junta losing power in 1983. In Thailand following the coup of 2006, the government's economic performance did not improve, which helped force its departure. In Tunisia and Egypt in 2011, inequality of economic opportunity played a major role in driving military-supported regimes from power. Both countries had enjoyed economic growth, but the benefits had not reached many in the country.

The collapse of the Soviet Union and the end of the cold war also played a major role in weakening dictator–armed forces alliances around the world. The greatest effect was in Central and Eastern Europe, where the retreat of the Soviet Union opened the way for a number of new democracies and for fundamental reform in the role of the armed forces. In Latin America, the suppression of Soviet- and Cuban-backed revolutionary movements in many countries had been part of the justification for autocratic, military-supported governments. After the cold war ended, the revolutionary movements collapsed, the violence abated, and the authoritarian regimes lost their support. In Africa what was seen as the triumph of the democratic model when the Berlin Wall fell led to dozens of multiparty elections, but without the other foundations for democratic governance, few led to sustained democratic change.

Globalization has had a positive effect on the spread of democracy and the weakening of military support for autocratic governments. Through freer flow of information worldwide, travel and contact among military officers, and both global and regional examples, a prevailing wisdom spread among most armed forces around the world, with the following tenets: the primary purpose of military forces should be defense against external enemies and support for internal economic development and safety; internal security roles are limited, temporary, and do not include using force against peaceful protests.

As of 2012, the number of authoritarian regimes with military support has been significantly reduced from its early 1970s peak. Freedom House has used consistent criteria to classify the state of freedom, which correlates with democracy, in all the countries of the world. Table 4-1 shows the progress that has been made from 1973 to 2012.

TABLE 4-1. State of Freedom, by Region, 1973 and 2012

Number

Region	1973			2012		
	Free	Partly free	Not free	Free	Partly free	Not free
Americas[a]	13	9	4	24	10	1
Asia[b]	9	11	11	17	14	8
Middle East and North Africa[c]	2	3	14	1	6	11
Sub-Saharan Africa[d]	3	9	28	11	18	20
Europe	18	4	25	37	10	7
Worldwide	45	36	92	90	58	47

Sources: Freedom House, "Freedom in the World 1973–2012" (www.freedomhouse.org/sites/default/files/FIWAllScoreRatings ByRegion1973-2012.xls; Freedom House, "Freedom in the World 2013" (www.freedomhouse.org/sites/default/files/FIW%20 2013%20Booklet%20-%20for%web.pdf).

a. Freedom House did not include Antigua and Barbuda, Bahamas, Belize, Dominica, Grenada, St. Kitts and Nevis, St. Lucia, St. Vincent and Grenadines, or Suriname in the 1973 report.

b. Freedom House counted North Vietnam and South Vietnam separately in 1973.

c. Freedom House broke Yemen into North Yemen and South Yemen for the 1973 report.

d. Freedom House did not include Angola, Cape Verde, Comoros, Djibouti, Eritrea, Guinea-Bissau, Mozambique, São Tome and Principe, Seychelles, or South Sudan in the 1973 report.

Future Challenges

For the armed forces of the established democracies, the challenge is both to start the remaining repressive regimes on the path to democracy and to support and strengthen the democratic development of those countries in transition.

In military relationships with the remaining authoritarian countries, the objective is to influence the armed forces to understand that their countries, services, and individual military leaders would better prosper in a democratic system. The ultimate goal is to bring them into the ranks of armed forces that are truly defending their people from harm, not supporting a government that someday will order them to fire on their fellow citizens. If the armed forces cannot become the agents of change, at least they should not be the opponents of change. Chapter 7 discusses potential approaches to take with several of the most repressive regimes: North Korea, Iran, Myanmar, Saudi Arabia, Pakistan, and China. Table 4-2 lists the remaining authoritarian countries. The armed forces of many of these

TABLE 4-2. Military-Supported Authoritarian Regimes, 2012

Region	Countries
Americas	Cuba
Asia	Cambodia, China, Fiji, Laos, North Korea, Vietnam
Middle East and North Africa	Bahrain, Iran, Saudi Arabia, Syria, United Arab Emirates, Yemen
Sub-Saharan Africa	Angola, Chad, Congo (Kinshasa), Congo (Brazzaville), Equatorial Guinea, Eritrea, Ethiopia, The Gambia, Guinea-Bissau, Mauritania, Sudan, Uganda, Zimbabwe
Europe and Central Asia	Azerbaijan, Belarus, Kazakhstan, Russia, Tajikistan, Turkmenistan, Uzbekistan

countries have military relationships with the armed forces of the democracies, and these connections can be used to influence military leaders in those countries.

In military relations with the transitional countries where democratic institutions, procedures, and culture have not been firmly established, the objective is to strengthen the democratic roles of the armed forces. Table 4-3 lists some of the countries that have started to move away from authoritarian regimes but in which democracy is not firmly established. Under these conditions, the challenge for the mature democracies is to use their influence with the armed forces of transitioning countries to help them establish a tradition of political neutrality and loyalty to the democratically elected civilian government and a primary mission of external defense, as well as laws and procedures in the key areas of civil-military relations, such as officer promotions, budget allocations, and legislative oversight.

The next chapter details how the armed forces of the mature democracies can foster democratic development through their existing relationships with both autocratic and transitional countries.

TABLE 4-3. Countries in Transition from Authoritarian Regimes, 2012

Region	Countries
Americas	Ecuador, Guatemala, Nicaragua
Asia	Afghanistan, Bangladesh, Indonesia, Myanmar, Nepal, Pakistan, Thailand
Middle East and North Africa	Egypt, Iraq, Kuwait, Lebanon, Libya, Morocco, Tunisia
Sub-Saharan Africa	Ivory Coast, Kenya, Niger, Nigeria, South Sudan
Europe and Central Asia	Kyrgyzstan, Ukraine

5

Outside Influences on Democratic Development

Several factors are important to the success of defense officials and military officers in democracies when trying to persuade their counterparts in autocratic countries of the advantages of a democratic system. First, their own democratic governments need to adopt a clear policy goal of supporting peaceful democratic transformation in autocratic or transitional countries around the world. Military organizations need straightforward guidance. The governments of established democracies must state explicitly to their departments of defense and their armed forces that one of the important objectives of interaction with foreign counterparts is to promote peaceful democratic development.

Currently, the established democracies are not clear and forthright about this policy goal. The Organization for Economic Cooperation and Development (OECD), for example, includes thirty-four countries, all democracies. When its Development Assistance Committee (DAC) published the *OECD DAC Handbook on Security System Reform,* it never clearly stated that the goal of security system reform in 2007 was to develop a country's armed forces within a democratic system of government.[1] Instead, it discussed helping countries "meet the range of security and justice challenges they face 'in a manner consistent with democratic norms and sound principles of governance and the rule of law.'"[2] There are extensive programs conducted by both NATO and less formal groupings of the established democracies to assist countries that have made a commitment to democratic reform and request assistance. However, what is lacking is a policy commitment by the democratic nations to use their relationships with authoritarian regimes to encourage peaceful democratic change. The latest National Security Strategy of the United States, published in 2010, reaches page thirty-seven of a fifty-two-page document before it states that "the United States supports the expansion of democracy and human rights abroad because governments that respect these values are more just, peaceful and legitimate."[3] Nowhere in this section of the document are military relations cited as an important tool in promoting democratic development. The official documents of other democracies are even more restrained. It seems to be considered unsophisticated and potentially offensive in policy circles to say openly and plainly that democracy is the best system of government and that democratic governments are in favor of more countries becoming democratic. Discussions of the issue in current policy documents are indirect and euphemistic. They need to be simple and direct.

Beyond policy documents, the established democracies are often reticent to advocate for democratic change when dealing with autocratic regimes rich in hydrocarbon or mineral resources (see box on p. 57). They should not be. It is important to emphasize once again that support for democracy means support for peaceful democratic transition over time, not for immediate, violent overthrow of dictatorships; the former has proved to be more durable, effective, and humane than armed insurrection.

Second, defense officials and military officers need to understand the state of democratic development in the countries with which they deal, and especially the state of support for democratic transition among the leadership and factions within the armed forces. Defense attachés and other specialists are generally knowledgeable on these issues, but the many other officers who deal with foreign counterparts must also learn the status of democratic development of the countries with which they deal if they are to be effective advocates for democracy. Service in the armed forces of a democratic state does not by its nature make an officer an expert, effective advocate and adviser for democracy in another country. Like other military activities, success in this kind of mission entails intelligence, education, planning, practice, feedback, and improvement. Senior officers dealing with other countries need to learn from attachés, regional experts, and intelligence officers about the democratic development issues in countries they visit and the personal roles in democratic development of counterparts with whom they deal. It is rare that an outsider can have a decisive influence on the decisions of a counterpart deeply involved in fundamental issues of military reform in an autocratic or transitional

Resource-Rich Repressive Regimes

Dictatorships with resources—Saudi Arabia, Kazakhstan, and Nigeria—are often treated with more deference than those without—North Korea, Zimbabwe, and Laos. However, this tendency is not universal. The United Nations has imposed tough sanctions on hydrocarbon-rich and autocratic Iran and Myanmar. However, the advanced democracies need to be clear and consistent that they favor the peaceful transition to democracy over time of even autocratic states with oil, natural gas, and mineral resources. This policy preference does not mean regime change through support for militant opposition groups or through direct military action; it means support for the components of democracy—rule of law, respect for minority and individual rights, a free press, and elections—and support for groups within these dictatorships that stand for peaceful democratic change. In their contacts with the armed forces of these countries, the military officers and defense officials of democratic countries should be direct and open about the advantages of a peaceful democratic transition of monarchies to constitutional monarchies and of dictatorships to democracies.

country, but if the individual is knowledgeable, he or she can encourage democratic behavior and discourage reversions to autocratic approaches. Appendix A provides a set of minimum intelligence requirements for all those with substantial responsibilities to interact with counterparts in autocratic or transitional countries, and a visiting officer should ensure that he or she knows the answers to all the questions posed in these intelligence requirements when dealing with foreign peers.

Third, democratic states need to collaborate in their approaches to supporting peaceful democratic change through military relations. Current efforts are ad hoc and uncoordinated, and amount to less than the sum of their parts in promoting democratic development. Different democracies have different strengths and weaknesses in their relations with

American and German soldiers help a Czech solider across an obstacle course. (DoD photo by Markus Rauchenberger, U.S. Air Force/Released)

autocratic countries around the world. French and British officers, for example, are seconded to serve in important assignments in the armed forces of some of their former colonies and
have many opportunities to help steer their comrades toward
democracy. Spain has unique influence among Spanish-speaking
Latin American countries. Australia deploys military advisers
widely through the South Pacific. Officers from newly independent countries in Africa, Asia, and Central and Eastern Europe
often have experiences more relevant to autocratic countries or
countries in transition than do those from the long-established
democracies. The United States spends the most money of any
country on specific programs of security assistance and carries
out a massive program of regular exercises with many countries
around the world.[4] Currently there are no established forums
in which the democratic countries of the world coordinate their
military relations to foster democratic development. NATO has
a well-established program called the "Partnership for Peace"
to provide assistance to countries that request it for education
of officers and defense officials and for program planning and
budgeting. These programs can strengthen democratic institutions in transitional countries but are not currently directed
toward influencing countries with autocratic regimes. In Africa
there are many security system reform programs in which
mostly European countries provide training and assistance
in many of the same areas. When there is an opportunity for
change, such as in Libya, there is intense ad hoc consultation
but rarely is there a history of contact with the autocratic country that would help the democracies know which officers and
officials should be supported and which should be opposed.
Overall, there is no sustained mechanism for the armed forces
of the established democracies to coordinate their programs
to develop democracy in specific authoritarian countries,
to exchange ideas on best practices for fostering democratic
reform, or to develop an overall approach that can be applied
to specific cases. With basic coordination among the ministries
of defense of these countries, different programs from different

countries can be applied to reinforce one another, greatly increasing their overall effectiveness. NATO and the Organization for Security and Cooperation in Europe (OSCE) are the existing organizations with the greatest membership of established democratic countries, and they are the best candidates to establish organizations and processes to promote democratic development through military relations.

"Policy Actions for Greater Effectiveness," below, summarizes the approaches needed to effectively advocate for democratic development among the militaries of transitioning and autocratic regimes.

Setting an Example, Discussion, and Persuasion

Any contact with a counterpart from an authoritarian country is an opportunity for influence. One of the most important ways to influence is by setting an example. Through their personal appearance, bearing, conduct and actions, officers and officials from democratic countries make an impression on

---

Policy Actions for Greater Effectiveness in
Promoting Democratic Development

➤ In the democratic countries, establish support for democratic
development as a primary mission for military relations with
autocratic and transitional countries.

➤ Within the armed forces of democratic countries, develop
detailed intelligence understandings of democratic development
within both transitional and autocratic countries.

➤ Establish international mechanisms within organizations such as
NATO or the OSCE for the armed forces of democratic countries
to coordinate activities that can support democratic change
through military relations.

their counterparts from autocratic countries. Some examples are small but telling: young People's Liberation Army officers have noted that senior officers from NATO countries are generally lean and physically fit, in contrast to many of their own overweight, sedentary generals. Foreign officers and noncommissioned officers are always interested in comparing salaries and are amazed by the size and reliability of compensation of their counterparts in democratic countries. These discussions are perfect opportunities to convey the respect that democratic countries have for members of the armed forces and the responsibility that legislatures in democracies have to provide adequate pay and benefits. Some opportunities are more important: visiting delegations from democracies that include civilian defense officials and military officers, and even officials from other executive branch departments and agencies like the State Department, demonstrate the mutual respect and teamwork that characterize civil-military relations in democracies. In their conversations with counterparts during visits, senior military officers can refer to the legitimate roles of appointed civilian defense officials and members of the legislature, and describe how they interact with them.

Both formal and informal conversations with counterparts in autocratic countries offer many opportunities for influence. The conversations among junior officers and noncommissioned officers participating in exercises and other security cooperation events become wide ranging as they work together over days or weeks. "How does this system work in your country?" is an introduction that can lead to fascinating conversations and opportunities for influence. Junior officers from democratic countries can convey the advantages of serving in the armed forces of a democracy: respect from their fellow citizens, adequate pay and benefits, merit-based advancement, and opportunities for employment after retirement. During the many opportunities for informal conversation, senior officers can directly discuss with their counterparts the larger issues of the role of military services in society: external defense as the primary role for the armed forces, the legal basis for operations both within and outside the country, the concept of legal orders, the advantages of a politically neutral role for the armed forces, and relationships with the legislature, especially as applicable to the budgetary process, and the press (see box below). In all of these conversations, the officers from democratic countries should seek to convey the system of laws and customs that underlies the respected institutional positions of the armed forces in a democracy, as well as the personal advantages of pay and benefits, respect for the uniform, and security enjoyed by the officer corps in democracies.

Visits to democratic states by military individuals and delegations from authoritarian countries are extremely important opportunities for influence by example. Based on their experience in their own countries, visitors from authoritarian states are suspicious of rehearsed demonstrations of capabilities and formal lectures. They have a keen and cynical awareness of political propaganda. They are more impressed by unrehearsed and spontaneous events from which they draw their own conclusions. The competence, initiative, and poise of noncommissioned officers and junior officers in the host countries, qualities that are developed naturally by democratic societies, convey the

---

Discussion Points with Counterparts in Nondemocratic Countries

➤ Relations with the public: respect for the military profession, assistance for those who leave military service, relations with the media, obligation not to participate in partisan politics.

➤ Military pay and benefits: adequate, covering family members as well as the service member; established by legislatures; corruption not tolerated.

➤ Internal defense responsibilities: always in support of police or other domestic agencies; temporary and extraordinary.

advantages of a democratic system, and opportunities can be created for this interaction. In the waning days of the cold war, Marshal Sergey Akhromeyev of the Soviet Union, during his visits to the United States, was impressed most by the junior personnel in the American armed forces, and even told his host Admiral William Crowe, chairman of the Joint Chiefs of Staff, that the Soviet system could not produce such fine junior personnel. Recreational and social events during visits should include civilian guests who can testify to the mutual respect between the citizens and soldiers of democratic countries. Senior foreign visitors can be introduced to military reporters, scholars in universities and think tanks, members of Congress and their staffs, and others to gain an understanding of the complex networks outside the military services that define the role of armed forces in a democratic society.

These opportunities for influence by example and discussion will have a cumulative effect on the officers and noncommissioned officers in dictatorships. In many cases, officers in the democracies form strong relationships with officers from autocratic countries that continue for years. The Internet has made these relationships much easier to maintain than in the past.

International Training and Education Courses

One of the most effective and important opportunities for influencing officers from autocratic countries occurs when they participate in military education and training courses presented in democratic countries. All the advanced democracies invite international officers to their military education institutions for courses of different durations. The experiences provided during these courses can have a powerful and positive effect on international students, both in terms of what they learn in the classroom and what they observe living and traveling in a democratic country.

The armed forces of less developed countries often send their most promising officers for education and training in the advanced democracies. Forty international students who attended the Army War College in Carlisle, Pennsylvania, went on to become the highest ranking general in their own armies. Over 600 of the international students of the Navy War College in Newport, Rhode Island, have become admirals. International military education and training is a valuable opportunity to influence the attitudes and understandings of future leaders of their armed forces. In addition to exposure to the advantages of democratic systems for both their services and their countries, they can learn from their fellow students the different forms that democratically established armed forces can take.

Although the international courses in the United States, NATO countries, and other mature democracies do not

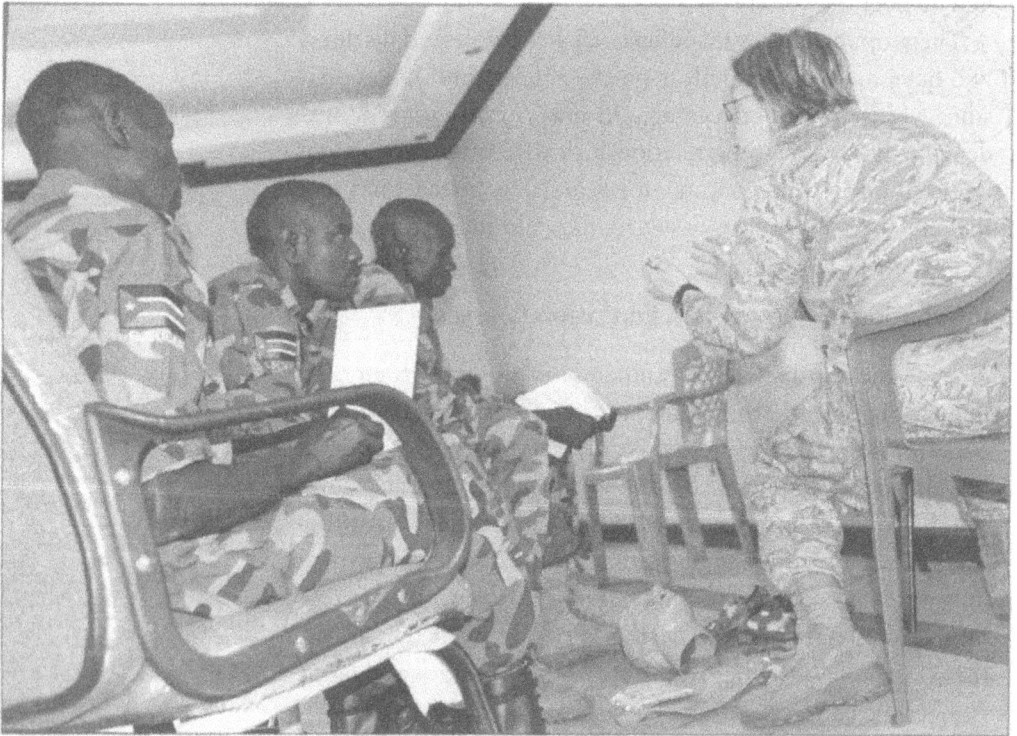

A U.S. Air Force physician's assistant discusses medical care with Southern Sudan soldiers in 2012. (DoD photo by Petty Officer 1st Class Justin Lewis, U.S. Navy/Released)

explicitly promote democracy as their major purpose, they incorporate related objectives. For example, the annual education and training report of the American Defense Security Cooperation Agency lists three goals for its international military education and training programs. The third is to "increase the ability of foreign military and civilian personnel to instill and maintain democratic values and protect internationally recognized human rights in their own government and military." The report goes on to state: "Training provided under the IMET [International Military Education and Training] program is professional and nonpolitical, exposing foreign students to U.S. professional military organizations and procedures and the manner in which military organizations function under civilian control."[5]

Many officers coming from autocratic countries have been profoundly influenced by the year they have spent, often with their families, in Carlisle, Pennsylvania, at the Army War College; in Shrivenham, Great Britain, at the U.K. Joint Services Command and Staff College; or at the Australian Defense College in Canberra. However, international students also criticize the limited manner in which the subject of the role of the armed forces in a democracy is taught. The emphasis in American war colleges is on explaining the American system, and a parallel focus applies in other countries. However, American or British customs and institutions tracing their lineage over two centuries and more are directly transferrable to very few other countries transitioning to democracy in the twenty-first century.

What is needed in these courses is a more universal discussion of the elements of the armed forces in a democracy, as explained in chapter 2 of this handbook, along with different examples, successful and unsuccessful, drawn from around the world. Seminars in which students from different countries compare their institutions and begin to understand the underlying common principles of the role of the armed forces in democracies would have a powerful effect. The observations of officers from countries that have made the transition to a democratic system more recently are often more relevant to attendees than the views of officers from long-established democracies. The objective of these essential courses in war colleges is to demonstrate that an effective democratic system can take different forms in different countries and to inspire officers from autocratic regimes to think about what form it might take in their countries. Appendix B provides a template for a seminar or a series of seminars for use in war college courses for international students.

According to surveys of international students, what they learn outside the classroom is as important as classes and seminars (see box on p. 67 for two examples). From experience in their own countries, military officers from authoritarian countries suspect that classroom instruction, especially on political topics like democracy, is biased. More compelling for them is what they learn from nonmilitary interaction with their civilian host families, what they observe on their field trips, and what they and their accompanying families experience in their local communities. Appendix C provides recommendations for components of field trips that will provide insights outside the classroom into the fundamental mechanisms that determine the place of the armed forces in democratic societies. A most important exposure would be to the role of legislative bodies like Congress or Parliament: international students should meet with the professional staff members of congressional or parliamentary armed forces oversight committees and with the elected members themselves. It is especially important to meet with staffs and members of the party out of power, demonstrating the bipartisan nature of military policy in democracies and the responsibilities of loyal opposition. Other elements of democratic societies that are important to understand include the media: military reporters, investigative reporters, editors, and television anchors. They also include professional civilian staff members of the U.S. Department of Defense or other ministries of defense, especially those officials who work in the areas of budget and personnel, and in the office of the general counsel. International students' field trips should include meetings with

Two Experiences with Training Courses

Lebanese Retired Brigadier General Edouard Abou Jaoude

Throughout his years as an officer, now-retired brigadier general Abou Jaoude attended an advanced training course with the U.S. armed forces in 2002 and a war college course with the Chinese military in 2008. He observed that during the U.S. training course, the officers were exposed not only to U.S. military procedures and technology but also American culture and values. These values include greater respect for human rights, religious and ethnic tolerance due to America's experience as a multiethnic democracy, freedom from torture, freedom of speech and the press, women's and children's rights, and the protection of minorities. Thus the education was not entirely focused on technical and military training but also on the important values that militaries should strive to protect.

In contrast, he found that the Chinese training course stressed theoretical technical military teaching and not the building of a cultural or personal relationship between the Chinese officers and the foreign officer students. Also during the Chinese war college course, there was never any mention of values of freedom, democracy, or human rights. General Abou Jaoude was also struck by the lack of military budget transparency and the lack of published information in China about military deployments and the People's Liberation Army's foreign contacts.

Lebanese Retired Colonel Nassif Obeid

Retired colonel Nassif Obeid had been an instructor at the Lebanese Military Academy before he attended an advanced training course in the United States in 1997 and a staff training course with the Syrian Armed Forces in 1999.

From his training course in the Unites States, Colonel Obeid realized that as a cadet in the military academy, he had been taught an authoritarian approach to leadership. He started working hard to change his way of thinking about leadership and succeeded with the help and influence of the U.S. instructors. Most important, Colonel Obeid learned during the U.S. training about the supremacy of the civilian population over any government. He learned that the priority for the armed forces is to protect the population against any harm, including from its own government.

During his staff training course in Syria, Colonel Obeid found that "the priority for the Syrian Armed Forces is to blindly obey the regime's orders and worship the dictator. The idea of citizen safety and rights is nonexistent." From these experiences, Colonel Obeid concluded that the essence of good military training is the positive shaping of officers to help them build character and a philosophy of leadership.

nonprofit organizations that address military issues—even those that cause problems for the armed forces by leaking sensitive information. Additional visits should include veterans' organizations, both government and private, as well as individual prominent veterans who have successfully moved into other fields when they left the armed forces. An important objective of these field trips is to expose officers from autocratic countries to the complex system of organizations, laws, and customs that underpin the role of the armed forces in a democracy.

In addition to six-month or year-long military education courses at war colleges and staff colleges for officers, the armed forces of democratic countries offer shorter training courses to both officers and senior enlisted personnel from authoritarian countries. Many of these courses are in connection with the sale of military equipment, while others are to build operational skills, from operational planning to small-unit tactics or even individual military skills, from maintenance to marksmanship. In general, these courses are functional, technical, and focused on military skills.

While these courses do not lend themselves to extensive instruction on the role of the armed forces in democracies, there is an opportunity to include content that emphasizes some of the elements of democratic armed forces. For operational planning courses, there should be instruction in the law of war—the justification for the use of force, proportionality, and avoidance of civilian casualties—and on working in international coalitions and with other countries, nonmilitary government officials, and nongovernmental organizations, both international and local.

For tactical courses, there should be instruction in the law of war at the unit and individual level—the right of self-defense, the principles of combatant status, and the treatment of enemy combatants and civilians. The Western Hemisphere Institute for Security Cooperation (WHINSEC), run by the U.S. Army, embeds training on these subjects in its extensive set of tactical courses for officers from Latin American armies. WHINSEC is the successor to the School of the Americas, which during the

1980s trained many officers from Latin American countries who were subsequently accused, and some convicted, of human rights abuses. However, the school has since examined its own record critically, has been extensively reformed and reorganized, and therefore is probably one of the most advanced institutions in teaching tactical military subjects under democratic conditions.

There are other education courses in democratic countries that are attended by midgrade and senior military officers and defense officials from authoritarian countries, and these also can influence attendees' thinking on democratic progress. For instance, the United States and Germany operate an extensive set of regional centers for security and defense studies; the first was the Marshall Center in Garmisch, Germany, launched in 1993. It was established for the education of officers and defense officials of the newly independent countries of Eastern Europe and the former Soviet Union as they reformed their defense establishments for entry into NATO. Based on the success of the Marshall Center, a counterpart center was established in Honolulu, Hawaii, for the Asia-Pacific region and three more were set up in Washington, D.C., for the Middle East, Africa, and the Western Hemisphere regions.

Each of these centers has a somewhat different focus, based on regional characteristics. The Marshall Center continues to offer a specific program on "Security Sector Capacity Building" that includes subjects such as "democratic control and oversight of the security sector." It also includes in its mission statement the objective of "advancing democratic institutions and relationships." The other centers do not emphasize the objective of developing democratic governance in their mission statements and courses, instead concentrating on common missions such as combating terrorism and drug cartels and on regional security issues.

There is an opportunity at the regional centers to increase the emphasis on development of democratic defense institutions. Seminars that address explicitly the role of the armed forces in a democracy could be adapted based on regional characteristics and contemporary events. Seminars on this subject would be extremely powerful because representatives from countries that are not democratic would interact with officials from many different democracies and countries in transition to democracy. The group discussion would have a powerful influence.

Two other useful American military courses offer instruction to officers of countries that have made the commitment to democratic development. The Defense Institute of International Legal Studies, in Newport, Rhode Island, offers a range of courses and sends traveling teams to give instruction to military lawyers of countries developing legal frameworks for their armed forces. The Center for Civil-Military Relations at the Naval Postgraduate School in Monterey, California, offers a variety of seminars and courses on reform of ministries of defense and uniformed forces to achieve both democratic norms and greater effectiveness.

Other established democracies have military education institutions with similar programs. The Defense Academy of the United Kingdom, located in Shrivenham, also has a long-established set of courses for international military students. The recently approved U.K. Defense Engagement Strategy recognizes the importance of international military education and is driving an expansion. For the academic year ending in 2011, the Defense Academy graduated students from ninety-three different countries and sent education teams to another thirty-five.

In the United States, Congress has often cancelled international military education and training for specific countries when it considers the human rights performance of that country's armed forces unacceptable. Historically, these actions have been counterproductive, diminishing American influence with the country concerned at just the time this influence is needed. It is true that the democratic countries should not continue business as usual with the armed forces of a country that are abusing their citizens. However, distinctions should be drawn between education, on the one hand, and training, on the other. It is certainly justifiable and effective to cancel arms sales and tactical training courses with a country when its armed forces are involved in brutal and repressive actions; however, educational courses are means to teach officers how mature armed forces in democracies conduct themselves. In fact, it is especially effective for them to be overseas when their home countries are acting in ways that attract international condemnation. When these officers return to their countries, they can be agents for change.

Multilateral and Bilateral Exercises

The armed forces of democratic countries conduct a wide range of exercises with the armed forces of authoritarian countries. Some are seminars on functional military subjects of common interest such as logistics, medicine, and peacekeeping tactics. There are also command post exercises, which are war games based on simulated scenarios, and field-training exercises, which involve tactical units maneuvering and firing on training ranges. Other types of exercises focus on additional military functions like support for humanitarian assistance and search and rescue operations.

The primary objective of multilateral exercises is to develop and refine the functional military skills that participating countries' military units expect to need in war, crisis, or peacetime operations, and to improve the ability to work together in these situations. Often the exercises are sponsored by alliances, such as NATO exercises conducted with forces from the Baltic states prior to their incorporation into the alliance, or based on traditional bilateral state-to-state relationships, such as U.S. exercises with the Philippines or French exercises with francophone African countries. At other times, the exercises are designed to develop the multilateral skills of UN-sponsored operations such as disaster relief and humanitarian operations and peacekeeping operations.

While it is not appropriate to conduct seminars on democratic transformation in connection with every international exercise conducted by a democratic country, there are many opportunities to introduce relevant democratic concepts. For example, humanitarian and disaster relief operations are complex and involve many nonmilitary participants: local government agencies, nongovernmental organizations, and local and international media. Multilateral military humanitarian and disaster relief exercises often include training seminars that cover relations with these other participants. These seminars can introduce or reinforce basic democratic concepts like subordination of military units to civilian government leadership, effective cooperation with civilian government and international nongovernmental organizations, and the importance of media transparency during military operations.

Even tactical military exercises with a combat focus present opportunities to teach or reinforce to officers and troops concepts such as the rights of noncombatants and other law of war principles. During peacekeeping exercises, participants from

Sailors from Mozambique and the Netherlands practice small-boat interdiction operations in 2012. (U.S. Air Force photo by Technical Sergeant Dan St. Pierre/Released)

democratic countries can introduce participants from autocratic countries to the concepts of armed forces operating under democratic principles.

Appendix D provides a checklist for the planning phase of exercises to cover the legal and democratic foundations for the use of armed force.

Multilateral and Bilateral Military Conferences, Seminars, and Visits

There is a well-developed schedule of conferences among the world's armed forces. Some are worldwide, such as the U.S. Navy–sponsored Global Naval Symposium; some are alliance based or regionally based, like the Pacific Special Forces Conference, along with literally hundreds of other bilateral conferences.

The conferences are often hosted by or include the significant participation of officers and civilian officials from the advanced democratic countries. Because they are attended by officers and officials from autocratic states or from countries in transition, they offer many opportunities for influence.

The conferences are generally organized around common missions performed by the participants; for example, there are continual conferences on peacekeeping operations, disaster response, search and rescue, and other "peace operations." There are also functional conferences and visits: service-to-service exchanges on logistics, special operations, marine salvage operations, military justice issues, communications, and dozens more.

Some of the seminars, on topics such as peacekeeping operations, military law, defense budgeting, and procurement, by their nature lead to discussions of the characteristics of defense forces in democracies. The participants from democratic countries must ensure that these characteristics are discussed and highlighted as "best practices." However, the most valuable opportunities offered by these kinds of activities are in the interactions that take place outside the formal settings.

The author remembers a conference of army chiefs of staff in the Asia-Pacific region in 1999, when the Indonesian Army was orchestrating or permitting attacks (it was never clear which) on civilians in East Timor. All the other army chiefs in their separate bilateral meetings with the head of the Indonesian Army took him to task for the failure of his troops to perform their duty of providing security for civilians in East Timor. Unwilling to endure more lectures from his peers, the general finally left the conference early. A few months later Indonesia agreed to an Australian-led United Nations force coming into East Timor.

Many of these discussions will take place spontaneously, as they did in the Indonesian case just cited. However, military officers from democratic countries are generally self-taught in these areas. No Australian, British, Japanese, or Korean officer considers the political control of the armed forces to be a major issue—it is the system in which he or she has always served—and he or she often has not given the concepts much thought. Officers and officials from the defense departments of democracies need to be reminded of the characteristics of the armed forces in a democracy (see chapter 2) and to be charged with the responsibility for raising the topics appropriately with their military colleagues from authoritarian countries. A starting point is the "elevator speech" described in chapter 1. In addition, the officers attending these conferences need to know the basic information about the degree of democratic development in the authoritarian countries of the officers they will be meeting. Appendix A provides a good starting point.

Bilateral visits are the most common points of contact between the officials of advanced democratic countries and officers and officials of authoritarian countries. Generally the representatives of authoritarian governments are well prepared in their formal meetings with talking points reflecting their government's position on a full range of issues, including a justification for their authoritarian form of government and for the roles of their armed forces in supporting those governments. Especially at senior levels, large portions of meetings are consumed by the recital of these points, which are then dutifully reported back to headquarters. While a meaningful exchange of real ideas is not likely in such settings, the officers from democratic countries need to be prepared to counter the points made by their authoritarian interlocutors with observations on both the favorable democratic trends in the world and the advantages to the armed forces of a democratic system. It has been the author's experience that in a surprising number of cases, senior officers from both authoritarian and transitioning countries will reply that a more democratic system is the goal for their country but that it will take time until the necessary conditions are achieved.

Opportunities for real dialogue arise in the more informal settings that form a large part of these visits—in cars between meetings, during dinners, or in waiting rooms when travel plans are changing. Over the course of a typical tour of duty

Opening ceremony of the multilateral exercise Cobra Gold in Thailand in 2010. (DoD photo by Cpl. Uriel De Luna-Felix, U.S. Marine Corps/Released)

for officers on both sides, which could span several years, multiple meetings form relationships in which these topics can be raised. Chance also plays a part—visits sometime occur when events force the discussion of these subjects, and there is a real opportunity to influence a counterpart to make a good decision for his service and country (see box below). In order both to create and to take advantage of opportunities to influence counterparts, officers from the established democratic countries need to prepare for this aspect of their visits as assiduously as they prepare for all other aspects. Briefings from intelligence officers and attachés on the state of democratic development within the country being visited and on the positions of individual senior officers with whom meetings are taking place can provide important information (see appendix A). Thus informed, each officer should then develop his or her own elevator speech based on the template described in chapter 1. Engaging in discussions of democratic development should be every bit as important a goal in bilateral visits as engaging in discussions about the policy question of the moment.

A Personal Vignette

Senior officers of the democratic governments are generally on their own in taking advantage of opportunities or in raising subjects to influence their counterparts from autocratic regimes. The author can recall visits during which senior officers with whom he had a relationship from authoritarian countries were wrestling with orders and policies from their dictator bosses. These senior officers were genuinely looking for advice and insight to help them make their decisions. The author, like most officers, knew the basic characteristics of armed forces in a democratic society but should have been far better prepared than he was to give advice and even to raise relevant topics when opportunities arose. It was this awareness of missed opportunities that motivated the writing of this handbook.

Arms Sales and Military Assistance

One of the strongest points of leverage that the advanced democracies have with the armed forces of autocratic governments or governments in transition are arms sales and military assistance grants. In the advanced democracies, decisions on arms sales to autocratic governments are made at the government level based on a balanced judgment of many factors. However, there are opportunities to use military assistance and arms sales to build democratic characteristics in autocratic and transitional countries making the purchases.

It would be powerful if an organization that includes most of the advanced democracies, like NATO or the OECD, were to adopt a set of requirements for purchasers of their arms or, failing that, a set of best practices. The requirements would ensure that even authoritarian governments satisfied certain minimum conditions of openness and transparency before they could buy weapons systems. Since the requirements would apply to all sellers from democratic countries, they would not advantage any one country.

However, even without a formal set of requirements, the advanced democracies can use their individual arms sales to move authoritarian regimes to more open defense practices. The types of arms sales and military assistance requirements, or best practices, that would support the long-term development of democratic conditions include the following criteria:

—The purchase of major equipment must be justified on the basis of an overall national defense strategy that is published in a defense white paper or other defense strategy document of the country making the purchase.

—The full and correct costs of contracts must be presented to and approved by the legislature of the purchasing government, and be published in the defense budget of the purchasing country.

—The recurring maintenance costs of equipment that is purchased must be included in defense budgets of the purchasing country, and the readiness condition of the equipment must be reported to defense ministries and to legislatures annually.

While it will be possible to fabricate phony responses to some of these requirements, and the legislatures and ministries of defense in authoritarian governments are often weak, rubber-stamp organizations, the process of meeting these requirements can lay the foundation for future defense reforms.

Unlike foreign equipment sales, in which the receiving country pays for what it purchases, foreign military aid is a grant to recipient countries. For foreign military assistance, the requirements levied by the providing democratic nation can be greater. If the conditions are not met, the grant can be withheld or suspended until they are.

For foreign military assistance in the form of equipment transfers, there should be a tailored set of requirements similar to those listed above for arms sales. Where there are no established planning and budgeting and accounting systems, the receiving country should be required to establish such a system, if necessary with the assistance of a program like the American Defense Resources Management Assistance Program. Another excellent source of defense management skills is the U.K. Defense Academy. Its faculty place special emphasis on teaching the practices and skills to eliminate corruption in equipment purchasing and other financial transactions of armed forces in developing democracies.

For foreign military assistance in the form of training and education, it is important that the officers who receive the education be upwardly mobile officers with career paths that take them into important senior positions. This requirement cannot be specified in billets and percentages, but it is possible to monitor over time whether the international students are in fact some of the best and brightest of their contemporaries, or whether authoritarian countries are sending intelligence officers or the students are officers who will never rise to leadership positions.

In applying these requirements, judgment must be used and a long-term view taken, as the circumstances in many individual countries are complicated. However, with arms sales and transfers, the objective is to create in recipient autocratic and transitional countries some of the processes that democratic governments apply in the acquisition of their own weapons systems. With education assistance, the objective is for as many as possible of the future real leaders of the armed forces of authoritarian countries and countries in transition to be given international military educations.

When Political Crises Arise

During political crises in dictatorships, the role of the armed forces is vital. If the armed forces support the regime against opposition, the regime will survive, at least for a time; if they do not, the regime will fall. The decision to sustain or withdraw support will be made by the senior leadership of the armed forces and generally involves a process of consultation within the officer corps. Generals do not want to give orders that their forces will not obey. Several of the case studies in volume 2 of this handbook describe crises in various countries when the role of the armed forces was crucial in deciding whether those countries would move toward democracy or not. The events of January and February 2011 are fresh in everyone's mind, when army leaders in Tunisia and Egypt made key decisions to withdraw their support from well-entrenched dictators.

During such political events, driven in part by media coverage, the full attention of the governments of democracies will be trained on the country in crisis. Presidents and prime ministers will set the policy, often making phone calls to counterparts and giving guidance to their cabinet officers and chiefs of service to contact their counterparts to urge the support of democratic development.

Probably the most powerful points that can be communicated to professional military officers in these circumstances have to do with duty, dignity, and legacy. Most successful military officers are deeply patriotic, wish to measure up to international standards of military leadership, and are concerned about how history will view their stewardship of their forces. A fellow military officer with whom they have a respectful relationship is the best person to persuade them to act honorably, both in everyday decisions and in the moments of crisis on the stage of his country's history.

Especially during a crisis, these points are best conveyed by a familiar voice, not some unknown person on a telephone line. Because of military rotation policies, officers with friends in autocratic countries in crisis may no longer be in a job with the formal responsibility for relations with that country. When there is a crisis, counterparts in the key jobs on both sides are often new, have not had the time to develop personal relationships, and can do no more than read their talking points to strangers. In these circumstances, especially with worldwide Internet and cell phone communications, there is a role for personal contact between officers in the advanced democracies who have already formed a relationship with officers in the authoritarian government in crisis. During the consultation period, officers from democracies should take the initiative to contact their friends in the autocratic countries to encourage them to support a preferred peaceful transition from dictatorship if possible, and one employing the minimal amount of necessary force.

Organizing this important outreach is complicated. The officer with personal contacts and influence should take the initiative, and the responsible staffs in the democratic countries need to be flexible in using these officers no matter what their rank or current assignments, including those that have retired. These officers should be brought into a virtual organization for the duration of the crisis. They should be provided with the latest intelligence, briefed on national policies and decisions, and used to contact their friends in other countries, both to urge honorable actions and to learn the state of play on the ground. This flexible organizational approach is no different from the joint task force principle that the armed forces use for plans and operations in all areas: define the mission, identify the personnel with the right skills, and place them in a temporary organization to accomplish the mission.

Whatever degree of organization is imposed on the process, officers and officials from democracies should be encouraged to communicate with their colleagues in autocratic or transitioning

countries, urging them to act to support democratic development in their countries during crisis, to refuse to obey orders
to attack their own citizens, and to be loyal to the long-term
interests of their country rather than to autocrats who oppress
the people.

Summary

Every point of contact between officers and officials of the
advanced democracies with an officer, official, or counterpart
in an autocratic country is an opportunity for influence. This
chapter has identified some of the most important and useful
opportunities: education and training courses, exercises, visits
and conferences, and arms sales. It includes recommendations
for using these opportunities to influence those from autocratic
countries to support a democratic transition in their own countries. These recommendations are only a starting point, however.
There are many additional and imaginative ways that the advantages of a democratic system can be demonstrated and conveyed
to military officers, appealing to their sense of patriotism and
sense of duty to the people they have pledged to defend.

Military-Military Relations during Violent Insurrections and Campaigns of Civil Resistance

As described in chapters 3 and 4, the long-term trend in world governance is toward more democracy. Dictators and one-party governments can hold onto power for a time—often a long time—but without the consent of their people and the capacity for renewal, they eventually crack and fall.

How they crack and fall matters. It has become increasingly clear in recent years that violent insurgencies almost never lead to a democratic outcome whereas successful nonviolent civil resistance movements have a high probability of creating durable democratic gains.

These results should not be surprising. The path to victory for a violent insurgency is military victory over a dictator and his supporters by force of arms. This process tends to concentrate power in the hands of those who engage in the violence, often men of fighting age who have little interest or stake in the frustrating realities of democratic governance. The violence imposes heavy costs on the rest of the population in the form of casualties, disruption and internal dislocation, and damage to the economy and critical infrastructure. The fighting, often savage and ruthless, weakens civil society, national unity, and rule of law. All these factors raise the odds against the establishment of democratic governance after the conflict.

In contrast, the objective of civil resistance is to weaken a dictator's support from the powerful groups on which he relies for control: the armed forces, government workers, businesses, and religious, cultural, and ethnic factions. Using protests, strikes, boycotts, and dozens of other tactics, opposition groups and ordinary people disrupt an authoritarian regime's rule, drive up the costs of maintaining the status quo, and ultimately convince regime supporters, including the armed forces, that the dictator can no longer run the country and therefore must go. Remaining nonviolent is crucial for an opposition movement to coopt the loyalties of a regime's supporters. Violence binds the latter closer to the regime, both because it threatens them with injury or death, and, in the case of the armed forces, it makes the opposition a more legitimate target for the use of military force.

American soldiers of the international peacekeeping force maintain crowd control as residents of Vitina, Kosovo, protest in the streets on January 9, 2000. (DoD photo by Spc. Sean A. Terry, U.S. Army/Released)

A 2005 study by Freedom House analyzed the results of revolutions over the prior third of a century. It found that in the twenty cases in which the freedom fighters used violence to remove a dictator, only five (25 percent) resulted in a free and democratic state following the end of the war. Of the twelve instances in which the freedom fighters used exclusively non-violent means, even though the government forces used violence against them, seven (58 percent) led to freedom and democracy. In the eighteen cases in which the transitions were entirely nonviolent on both sides, seventeen (94 percent) achieved both freedom and democracy.[1]

Armed Insurrection

Armed rebellions are common throughout history and continue to the present. They have ended in recent years in Mexico, Nepal, Libya, and the Philippines, and continue, as this chapter is being written, in Syria, the Democratic Republic of the Congo, India, and Yemen.

Security forces know how to deal with armed threats to their countries, whether from outside or within. When armed rebels attack army outposts, soldiers defend the outpost and then pursue the armed enemy. When armed rebels capture control of towns or territory, government armed forces plan and execute campaigns to regain control. It is rare for an army to disobey orders—even from a despot—to suppress an armed rebellion and rare, for a period of time at least, for the population not to support the armed forces and the government. Often the government and its forces are ultimately successful in defeating armed opposition. A 2011 study that reviewed 218 cases of violent insurrectionary campaigns challenging governments between 1900 and 2006 found that the governments suppressed 74 percent of them.[2]

The regional surveys and case studies in volume 2 of this handbook provide several important examples of the range of outcomes of armed revolutionary movements, successful and unsuccessful. Outright victories of insurgent armed forces seem rarely to lead to democratic government. In Angola, Mozambique, and Zimbabwe, freedom fighters became dictators. Tanzania is the only post–armed revolt African country that has moved toward democracy, although the journey is not yet complete. In Indonesia and Vietnam, the victorious revolutionary forces replaced Dutch and French colonial rule with military-supported local dictatorships. Armed revolutions in Iraq, Syria, and Egypt all brought dictators to power in place of colonial rule. In Cuba the dictator Fidel Castro replaced the dictator Fulgencio Batista, whom he had deposed.

In cases where the government forces were successful in suppressing armed revolt, widening of democratic governance when the violence ended was a key to sustaining the victory. Military defeat of an armed insurgency followed by continued autocratic rule generally has meant continued revolt. In Latin America in the 1970s and 1980s, revolts were put down in Chile, Peru, and Argentina, but it was not until autocratic rule peacefully ended that these countries enjoyed stable conditions. In Asia the Philippine government has contained armed resistance in its southern islands but has not been able to end the dissatisfaction and support for armed revolutionaries by its disenfranchised Muslim citizens. The Indonesian government similarly contained revolt in East Timor for decades and continued suppressing armed resistance until its first democratically elected president decided to grant East Timor independence. In Africa military victories by dictators have led to temporary periods of peace but few long-term stable environments.

A third durable outcome of armed revolution has been negotiated settlement without victory by one side or the other. In the cases of El Salvador and South Africa (described in volume 2), the outcomes were political peace settlements after years of bloody but indecisive conflict. This was also true for Nepal. In all three countries, the armed forces were reconstituted by combining soldiers from both the former government forces and the revolutionary forces into a new security force.

External influences on armed revolts take the form of support for either government forces or the rebels. Outside countries make national level decisions about which side to support and what degree of assistance to provide. To cite contrasting recent examples, the members of NATO decided to support the government of Afghanistan against the Taliban rebel forces and have provided huge amounts of military assistance. The same countries decided to support the armed opposition against the government of Libya and provided it with military support.

The basic mission of military officers from the mature democracies deployed to countries fighting violent civil wars is set by national policy. However, whether they are supporting government or rebel forces, military advisers strongly influence their counterparts, and they can make a difference in whether a violent civil war results in a democratic country or a dictatorship.

The *U.S. Army/U.S. Marine Corps Counterinsurgency Field Manual* provides guidance when the United States is supporting a legitimate government against challenge by a violent insurrection. It provides excellent detailed instructions for counterinsurgency operations but falls short in specific guidance for strengthening democracy while supporting a government. It states unequivocally: "The primary objective of any [counterinsurgency] operation is to foster development of effective governance by a legitimate government."[3] The manual avoids using the word "democracy" but defines a legitimate government as one that provides "a high level of popular participation in or support for political processes."[4] That is close enough. However, in chapter 6 of the field manual ("Developing Host-Nation Security Forces"), even in the section entitled "Training Leaders," there is no discussion of developing the understanding of the role of the armed forces in a democracy: defending the people, the military contribution to society, and the importance of reconciliation and reintegration for the long-term democratic and peaceful development of a country.[5] These are important omissions, as the foundation for enduring free and democratic societies needs to be laid during the violent phase. Moreover, as many of the case histories in volume 2 of this handbook show, military officers of the victorious side will play some of the most important roles in deciding the shape of the government that emerges from the conflict. Both in formal education courses and, probably more importantly, in informal conversations, advisers and trainers from the democratic countries should convey the principles of the armed forces in a democratic country to their military counterparts.

For the same reasons, and perhaps more urgently, when the armed forces of the established democracies are supporting an armed rebellion against a dictator, it is vital for outside advisers to influence their counterparts about the government that will emerge when the rebels win. The greatest recent failure on this score occurred during the 1980s Soviet war in Afghanistan, when the United States supplied weapons to the *mujahideen*, enabling their military victory, then walked away from the country, leaving the victors they had backed to establish their own even more repressive regime. More positively, in Libya at the time of this writing, the democratic governments that assisted the Libyan rebel forces have remained engaged and are helping with the formation of democratic institutions.

The Armed Forces and Campaigns of Civil Resistance

Campaigns of civil resistance have deep historical roots. Civil resistance was used to wrest political reforms from Tsarist Russia in 1905, to achieve India's independence between 1930 and 1947, and by Martin Luther King Jr., to challenge systematic oppression in the American South in the 1960s. It also catalyzed the downfall of the Marcos regime in the Philippines in 1986, contributed to the end of Augusto Pinochet's regime in Chile in 1988, enabled Poles to weaken and end Soviet control between 1980 and 1989, and played a prominent role in antiapartheid resistance in South Africa in the 1980s. More recently, Serbs nonviolently overthrew the rule of Slobodan Milosevic (2000), Ukrainians successfully reclaimed a stolen election (2004), and millions of citizens successfully engaged in civil resistance in Tunisia and Egypt during the Arab Awakening. In all these instances, other factors played important roles, but the skillful use of civil resistance by opposition forces was decisive.

There is a well-developed literature about grassroots movements and their use of civil resistance to create political, economic, and social change. Prominent thinkers such as Gene Sharp, Peter Ackerman, and others have developed political theory and strategic insight on how movements effectively engage in civil resistance, while scholars such as Erica Chenoweth have done compelling quantitative studies showing the efficacy of this means of struggle. Most recently, Chenoweth reviewed 105 civil resistance campaigns challenging governments between 1900 and 2006 and found an aggregate success rate of 53 percent for those campaigns.[6]

Opposition movements engaged in civil resistance have learned the importance of dealing directly with military leaders and units to undercut their support for authoritarian regimes. Two of the most successful instances in recent years were in

Leaders from the protest movement and the army had been in contact for two years before the decisive demonstrations in Ukraine in 2004. (Photo by Neiljs/Flickr)

Serbia in 2000 and Ukraine in 2004. In both cases the opposition movements stressed publicly their patriotism and respect for the armed forces and called on the armed forces to serve the people, not the dictator. In Ukraine, the opposition movement enlisted a sympathetic retired general to establish direct communications with senior military officers to gain commitments that the army would not use force against mass demonstrators. More recently, in both Tunisia and Egypt, opposition leaders were careful to show their respect for the armed forces and have called on them not to use force against their own people. This is a powerful appeal to service members of all ranks, touching their basic motivations for joining the armed forces.

Outside influences can also play a role during civil resistance campaigns, and defense officials and military officers can influence their counterparts to refuse to implement violent suppression measures against them. The first requirement is that the democratic governments themselves have clear policies of supporting nonviolent change toward democracy. The records of the leading democratic countries during the events of the Arab Awakening have been mixed. Eventually, the leading democracies came down on the side of democratic change. However, their noticeable silence on the actions of the Bahraini government and early hesitations concerning other countries undercut the later public statements of support for democratic transitions.

To repeat the point made earlier in chapter 5, the established democracies should state clearly and firmly that they favor nonviolent democratic change in all autocratic countries, even if they have oil and mineral resources or are staunch allies against al Qaeda. This policy does not mean that democracies are working for quick regime change in every country where there is a protest against a dictator. However, it does mean calling on autocratic governments to listen to their citizens' concerns when they engage in civil resistance, to allow greater participation in government, and to refrain from using violence against nonviolent protesters.

Within this policy framework, the military officers of the democracies can influence their counterparts in autocratic countries to support the people, not a dictator. In the early days of the Arab Awakening protests in Egypt in 2011, a senior Egyptian military delegation happened to be in Washington on an official visit. During their meetings, senior American counterparts had the opportunity to discuss directly with them the importance of the Egyptian Army in maintaining order without using force against protesters.

During political crises of this type, it is typical for senior military officers from democracies, at the direction of their governments, to call their counterparts to try to persuade them not to use force to suppress acts of civil resistance, such as protests, strikes, boycotts, or other disruptive but nonviolent tactics. This type of lecturing is fine as far as it goes, but it does not go very far. Far more effective would be for the officers from democracies to discuss with their counterparts how it is in both their personal and their service's best interests to remain loyal to the people and the country rather than an autocratic ruler, using the arguments suggested in chapter 1. This type of an appeal to a counterpart's personal interest and the long-term interest of his service is much more powerful. Such conversations would be even more effective if they occur between officers in key command positions who have a preexisting, collegial relationship. Because officers rotate to different assignments every few years, it is rare for senior officers in a democracy to form friendships of any duration with their institutional counterparts in other countries. However, at least some friendships will have been formed over the years among different officers in the democracies and autocratic states. When a political crisis erupts, those officers and defense officials should be encouraged to communicate with their friends in the autocratic country in crisis to urge them to act in the best long-term interests of their services and their country, and not to support dictators who have lost popular support. Under these circumstances, such officers should be aggressive in initiating communications with their friends in the autocratic countries. Staff at the command headquarters of the democracies should quickly bring these officers, who may have unrelated current assignments, into the official efforts to influence autocratic countries in crises. These officers, through their contacts, will be able to provide unique and accurate information on developments and will also be able to assert a personal influence on their counterparts. (For an example, see "Right Place, Right Time," below)

Giving advice like this to senior officers in autocratic countries undergoing political crises is not something to be done lightly. If opposition movements engaged in civil resistance prevail, then the military leader who defied his own government and stood by the people is a hero, as is General Rachid Ammar of Tunisia today for refusing his president's order to send soldiers against protesters. However, if a government overcomes

Right Place, Right Time

In January 2001, the author was the commander-in-chief, U.S. Pacific Command, and was in Manila on a previously scheduled official visit. The impeachment trial of Philippine president Fernando Estrada was coming to a head, and huge crowds were demonstrating in Epifanio de los Santos Avenue (EDSA) for him to resign. The author had formed a friendship with the chief of the armed forces of the Philippines, General Angelo Reyes, over the course of several years. During a meeting in his office, General Reyes showed the author an order he had just received from President Estrada to deploy army units to clear EDSA, using force if necessary. "What should I do?" asked General Reyes. The author replied that General Reyes should not follow the order because he did not want to be known as the general who had ordered his troops to stand against the people. "But what do I tell the president?" General Reyes asked, a reasonable question. After a few minutes of discussion, General Reyes decided that he should send the order to the Philippine supreme court for an opinion on its legality. Within days General Reyes informed President Estrada that the army no longer supported him, and the president resigned.

the opposition's civil resistance, then military leaders who did not follow orders will certainly lose their positions, and perhaps their liberty and lives. Both military leaders in dictatorships and their friends in democratic countries must decide if a civil resistance movement opposing the government is strong and skilled enough to prevail against the dictatorship. If the movement is broad based, and if its leadership is competent and dedicated to democracy, then it deserves the support of patriotic military leaders. If these characteristics have not developed, a civil resistance movement still may be worthy of support, but the risks of failure and of renewed authoritarian rule are high.

Summary

The historical record shows that nonviolent civil resistance is the most effective method to end autocratic regimes and replace them with durable democratic governments. The established democracies should support serious and principled nonviolent civil resistance wherever it is challenging dictators, and should support negotiations between dictators and civil resistance movements to forge new democratic forms of government.

One of the major objectives of a civil resistance movement will be to undercut the support of the armed forces for a dictator. When a civil resistance movement reaches an effective level, the developed democracies, through all means including military interactions with counterparts, should influence the dictator's army to withdraw support from the dictator in favor of the establishment of a democratic form of government.

When the armed forces of the established democracies are providing assistance to either government or rebel forces in a violent rebellion, they should influence counterparts to establish democratic governance at the end of the violence. The path to democratic governance includes negotiated agreements, integration of armed forces from government and rebel units, as well as establishing or strengthening the seven elements of the armed forces in a democracy, described in chapter 2.

7

Hard Cases

This chapter addresses military relations with several important autocratic countries that are difficult to move toward democracy: North Korea, Iran, Myanmar, Saudi Arabia, Pakistan, and China. Conventional wisdom has been pessimistic that any of them can change. However, in the past, dictators who have seemed solidly in control of their countries, supported slavishly by armed forces and other security services, have toppled with astonishing speed, and the leaders of armed forces have in many cases shown them the door. While this handbook was being written, Myanmar moved away from its autocratic past with surprising speed.

It is important to acknowledge at the outset that the most important factors that cause autocratic regimes to change or to relinquish power are internal. Most common are splits within the leadership or poor economic performance. External factors, including military influences, play a secondary role. Nonetheless, the established democracies should use every tool of influence they have with autocratic regimes to induce them to move in a democratic direction and should refrain from policies or actions that provide them with encouragement or justification to remain as they are.

The established democracies have a range of military relations with the six countries listed above. Military relations with

Iran, North Korea, and Myanmar are minimal, whereas military relations with Saudi Arabia, Pakistan, and China are wide ranging. Relations with each of the six vary among the democracies. For example, the United States has the closest relationship with Saudi Arabia, while the Republic of Korea has the closest connection with China. It is important for each country to use the influence it has and to coordinate with the other democracies to maximize the effect of their common efforts.

North Korea

The touch points with the potential to influence North Korea through military relations are very few. The regime's relations with the democracies of Asia are generally so hostile that not even the routine cooperative military arrangements such as search and rescue and humanitarian assistance exist. Despite North Korea's "military first" policies and the martial trappings that surround its public events, the Kim family dictatorship has always followed the communist tradition of keeping close watch on the loyalty of its armed forces through a separate intelligence service and through frequent rotations of senior officers to prevent them from accumulating power and becoming potential rivals. There have been scattered reports over the years of unrest and even revolts by individual military units, but none has been successful.

By all objective measures, the Kim regime, now starting its third generation, has been a failure. The economy and population have shrunk in recent decades, and the lives of the great majority of North Koreans are grim. Only the repressive measures of a police state and the support of the power elites have kept the Kim family in control. With the upsurge of North Koreans fleeing their country, and the penetration of cell phone service from China into regions of the country, ordinary North Koreans are increasingly realizing how backward and repressed their country is. Elites with access both to cell phones and to television broadcasts from South Korea, China, and other countries by satellite understand how poorly their country measures up by all standards of development. Regimes like Pyongyang's are strong but brittle, and once a split develops among the tight ruling group, the end will come quickly.

The only democracy that has a military relationship with North Korea is Mongolia, which signed a defense agreement with the Democratic People's Republic of Korea in 2008. Any contact between Mongolian defense officials and military officers with their North Korean counterparts should have a positive effect. In their interactions with Mongolians, the North Koreans cannot help noticing that an independent and democratic Mongolia is taking full advantage of its relations with the developed world to generate an 8 percent economic growth rate. Perhaps through contact with Mongolian officers and other sources of information from the outside, North Korean

Two North Korean guards looking south across the demilitarization zone. (U.S. Army photo by Edward N. Johnson)

military officers can realize that their country could improve its economy and the lives of its citizens by becoming more democratic. Under those circumstances, the North Korean armed forces could help and could defend their fellow citizens, without having to live off their imposed sacrifices.

Realistically, however, the armed forces of the democracies, including Mongolia, currently have little influence with their counterparts in North Korea except to deter them from rash acts of aggression. Nonetheless, if there is an indication of change in Korea, opportunities for influence will appear suddenly, as they have in Myanmar recently. The armed forces of South Korea will be the best placed and most influential military officers from a democracy to win over the armed forces of North Korea, and they should take the lead for coordination with other democratic armed forces to plan for influencing military officers in North Korea when a crisis occurs.

Iran

The Iranian regime is intensely suspicious of outside influences and severely limits the contacts of its military personnel with those from the democracies, which are considered hostile and subversive. There is little opportunity for exerting influence through military relations.

Although outside countries have little influence on the dynamics of the relationship, they should pay close attention to the differences and rivalries between the regular Iranian forces and the increasingly powerful and corrupt Islamic Revolutionary Guard Corps (IRGC). The clerical regime relies ever more heavily on the IRGC for its support. It was the IRGC and its auxiliary militia, the Basij, that suppressed the protests following the 2009 election. The regime is rewarding the IRGC by giving its leaders control of monopoly businesses in key sectors, including oil and gas. Meanwhile the Iranian army, suspected in the past of pro-Shah sympathies, has been losing funding and is subjected to much tighter political control from the government than the IRGC.

The most likely cause for political change in Iran is division within the leadership groups. In addition to the disputed 2009 election, there has been a contest for power over the past year between President Mahmoud Ahmadinejad and Supreme Leader Ali Khamenei in which the latter has prevailed. Yet Supreme Leader Khamenei has rivals within the theocracy that rules Iran, and the regime's support among the general population is not firm and widespread. Should a political crisis arise in Iran, the IRGC and the regular armed forces may well support different sides. The democracies and their armed forces should be ready to exploit these divisions as the opportunity arises and to support the factions with allegiance to the country of Iran and its people, not to the clerical dictatorship.

Myanmar

Since independence on January 4, 1948, the armed forces of Burma (since 1989 also known as Myanmar) have constantly operated on a war footing, usually in a context of emergency, in significant portions of national territory and against forces financed, trained, or otherwise intermittently supported by at least five foreign governments (United States, China, Thailand, India, and the United Kingdom). During the 1950s, civil wars were fought mainly in central Burma for control over the government based in Rangoon. During that period, the military came to view itself as the "defender of the nation" and as more disciplined, conscientious, and patriotic—and thus better equipped to hold the country together—than squabbling civilian politicians, former comrades-in-arms in the anticolonial movements of the 1930s. Military leaders gradually eliminated the prerogatives of elected politicians to oversee national security affairs; moved the armed forces into large-scale commercial enterprises, ranging from local businesses run out of garrisons to cabinet–ministerial level firms; and eventually seized direct political power for the first time in 1958.

By the 1960s, the central regions were pacified, but the internal threats shifted to the ethnic-nationality-dominated territories along Burma's international borders, where a confusing array of armed antistate groups, fielding tens of thousands of soldiers, fought for autonomy or secession, mostly in the name of minority grievances and identity claims. In the 1990s, the junta and many of those groups entered into temporary cease-fire arrangements, a handful of which transformed into mutually acceptable political institutions under the 2008 constitution. However, the largest, most strategically important cease-fires have broken down repeatedly in recent years, and the army is reengaged in a full-scale war in much of northern Myanmar.

No foreign military or foreign government has ever had any significant influence over the behavior, policies, and actions of the postcolonial armed forces of Burma/Myanmar. The drivers of political change and institutional reforms are not the generals' concerns for domestic legitimacy, international reputation, or even foreign investment but rather the Tatmadaw's (the Armed Forces' or junta's) assessments of internal security threats and internal military-institutional politicking.

The current political reforms in Myanmar are based on the 2008 constitution, which took fifteen years to write under a tightly controlled process. The document strongly protects the importance, prerogatives, and independence of the armed forces. However, it introduces a division of labor, allowing the government to enact policies and laws, as well as to implement, enforce, and adjudicate them, on matters considered not directly relevant to national security. Although there has been no major shift in the characteristics of who rules (ethnic Burman active duty or retired military officers), a new political system is emerging that is changing how they rule. Simply put, Myanmar appears now to differentiate the armed forces' command structure from administration and governance.

This new constitution and the early actions of President Thein Sein are heartening changes in Burma. They should be encouraged by the established democracies using a carefully considered set of military-military relations.

A few basic principles should guide any future engagement. The Myanmar Defense Services take credit for transitioning from a national crisis (1988) to junta rule, and then on to the "genuine, disciplined multi-party democratic system" espoused under the 2008 constitution.[1] Hence, military-to-military engagement should not use the rhetoric of "inculcation of democratic values," which will be seen by Burmese officers as yet another series of paternalistic, neocolonial initiatives or even threats. Programs aimed at promoting human rights and democratic civilian control of the military should take a long-term view regarding outputs or effectiveness. Burma/Myanmar has never really had any civilian control of its military, there is no such thing as a "civilian defense" official or bureaucrat, and no foreign military or government has ever had any significant impact on major intramilitary policies. In this context, there can be no simple one-size-fits-all democratization formula.

Given this new window of opportunity, for the next several years, the most valuable forms of military engagement will be high-level exchanges of visits with Myanmar military leaders both to reward the early reforms and to exchange ideas for the future; education of promising mid-grade officers through attendance at the military colleges in democratic countries, and assistance to military education in Myanmar itself (President Thein Sein was commander of the Myanmar Defense Services Academy); and capacity-building programs for officials of the ministries of defense, home affairs, and border areas. As relations progress, and if positive developments continue in Myanmar, a range of activities can be considered to bring Myanmar's armed forces into the international military activities devoted to common missions—search and rescue, disaster response, maritime security, and UN peace operations. In addition, a coordinated, sequenced, and reversible plan should be developed among the democracies to wean Burma off its dependence on China, Russia, North Korea, and the black market for its military equipment. Whatever engagement with the Myanmar Tatmadaw is undertaken, it should be reversible, given that there is no guarantee that the present set of political reforms and warming of relations between Myanmar and the democratic countries will continue along the same path.

Saudi Arabia

Saudi Arabia is an absolute monarchy, with the government ruling by decree. The regime continually announces, and sometimes actually takes, small steps to establish more democratic institutions—judicial reform, municipal elections, and more rights for women—but they are very modest, and the king retains power. Its oil wealth provides King Abdullah the means to ensure material well-being for the royal family and the power elites and to increase payments to any groups of Saudi citizens showing dissatisfaction. Thus, as democratic reform and the departure of dictators swept the Arab world in 2011, there were no major protests in Saudi Arabia. Still, the regime announced

Saudi Arabia's King Abdullah receives former U.S. Defense Secretary Robert Gates, left, as Ambassador to the United States Adel Al-Jubair, center, translates at Riyadh Palace in Riyadh, Saudi Arabia, April 6, 2011. (DoD photo by U.S. Air Force Master Sgt. Jerry Morrison)

a substantial increase in the pay of civil servants and other subsidies to Saudi citizens.

Surrounded by countries in which military coups have been common, the Saudi monarchy divides military power among independent security organizations, each with its own royal leader. The regular armed forces report to the defense minister; the Saudi Arabia National Guard (SANG), with units as capable as those in the regular army, reports to a separate prince; and the police and intelligence services report to the minister of the interior. Domestic security is entirely the responsibility of the minster of the interior, so neither the regular forces nor the SANG are called on to repress the population.

The armed forces of the advanced democracies, especially the United States, have long and deep contact with both the regular Saudi armed forces and the SANG. Saudi officers are both educated and trained in the United States, exercise with American units, and were wartime allies during the first and second Iraq wars. The armed forces of the United Kingdom, France, and other European countries also have long and close ties with the Saudi armed forces.

With all these touch points, why have the advanced democracies not been able to influence Saudi Arabia to implement democratic reforms? Why have the Saudi armed forces not adopted the values of the democratic armed forces from whom they buy their weapons systems, with whom they have fought, and by whom they have been educated and trained?

Part of the reason is that the democracies need Saudi Arabian oil. In addition, Saudi Arabia has been an ally of the United States and the European democracies in offsetting Iranian influence in the region, removing Saddam Hussein from power, and suppressing al Qaeda, which was led by the Saudi-born Osama bin Laden. With major interests like these in common, the democracies have judged it not worth the risk of pushing political change with the Saudi regime.

Even without formal pro-democracy government policies toward Saudi Arabia, it would seem that the years of contact would have produced a desire among some influential Saudi military officers for their country to move toward a more democratic government. This has not happened. Part of the reason is that the Saudi government is aware of the potentially subversive effect of too much exposure to democratic countries and therefore controls the number of officers sent abroad. Even more important, it seems that Saudi officers, despite their extensive interaction with the armed forces of the democracies, in general have not seen either a need or applicability for democratic concepts in their own country. As one keen observer has written, "Saudi personnel, coming from a very conservative society, did not relinquish their beliefs [when they were exposed to Western democratic ideas] but, through the exposure, developed a better understanding for the way of life and values of other people, ensuring respect, a positive view, and openness to other cultures and norms."[2]

The armed forces of the democracies will continue to have a full range of interactions with their Saudi counterparts in the future. Although there is little likelihood that these interactions alone will move Saudi Arabia toward democracy any more than they already have, they will continue to prepare the ground for the transition that eventually will come. American dependence on Saudi oil is diminishing, and technology will eventually find replacements for petroleum-based transportation sectors in developed countries. However, in the near term, the United States and the other democracies will continue to see Saudi Arabia as the swing supplier to the international oil market and a bulwark against Iranian influence, and will also continue to value Saudi Arabian assistance against al Qaeda. It is not likely they will risk these important interests by aggressively encouraging political change in Saudi Arabia.

Nonetheless change will come to the Kingdom of Saudi Arabia, whether it wishes it or not. As the events of the past year in many other Arab countries have shown, Arabs value their personal dignity and want to choose their own leaders as much as anyone. In 2011 Saudi military units, along with those from Gulf states, complied with orders from their governments to enter Bahrain to suppress protests by Shia groups in Bahrain.

However, they will find it more difficult to turn their weapons against fellow Sunnis who protest against oppression by the Saudi government. Other, younger Arab kings in Jordan and Morocco have realized they need to move toward constitutional monarchies, share power with elected legislatures, and allow the formation of loyal opposition parties. Saudi Arabia can be encouraged to follow this trend, and in their military relations with Saudi Arabia, officials and officers from the established democracies can encourage their Saudi counterparts to support peaceful, positive change.

Pakistan

Pakistan has all the elements of a democratic government, and some of them are partially effective, but it faces many obstacles in developing the reality of a functioning democracy. One of the greatest obstacles is the Pakistani army, which can remove the elected government at will, controls the country's security policies entirely, heavily influences many domestic policies, and is largely financed by commercial enterprises it controls. Its intelligence organization operates throughout the country with wide powers of investigation, arrest, and detention.

The Pakistan Armed Forces have maintained strong, if often antagonistic, relationships with the armed forces of many democracies, especially the United States. For the past decade, the military relationships with the United States and other NATO members have intensified, centered on the NATO operations in Afghanistan and the campaign against al Qaeda. Meanwhile, Pakistan has been dealing with a succession of political crises, economic stagnation, and rising levels of violence both in the Federally Administered Tribal Areas in the northwest and in other regions, including Karachi.

Senior Pakistani officers are very familiar with the attributes of the armed forces in a democratic system of government. Many have studied in military colleges in democratic countries; they have participated in international training exercises and peace-keeping operations, and information on the rest of the world is freely available in Pakistan. However, if anything, the general opinion of the United States and the other established democracies has deteriorated among Pakistani officers, making them less favorably inclined toward a similar democratic system for their own country. There are several reasons. First, the United States has placed heavy pressure on Pakistan and its army to divert resources from the mission of confronting India to suppressing the radical Islamic groups operating in northwest Pakistan. Pakistanis generally regard this as an American security agenda that does not match their own. Second, the United States has recognized India's nuclear weapons while still questioning the safety and security of Pakistan's weapons. Third, in its campaigns against both al Qaeda and the Taliban, U.S. forces have violated Pakistani sovereignty on repeated occasions. Fourth, Pakistani officers are suspicious that the United States will lose interest in Pakistan, as it did following the intense cooperation of the 1980s Afghan war against the Soviet Union. These days American-style democracy is a hard sell to Pakistani military officers.

Ironically, while the Pakistan Armed Forces have become more hostile toward the United States, the U.S. government, by the way it has conducted its relations with Pakistan, has increased the authority of the army within the country. Recognizing the reality of the army's power in Pakistan, American administrations have fallen into the habit of using their own military leaders to deal directly with the Pakistani army leadership on national security questions. Americans actions have treated it as a more important channel than communications with Pakistani civilian government leaders. This practice has deeply undercut the authority and legitimacy of the civilian government in Pakistan, and elevated the importance of the army and its unelected leaders. In summary, the last decade of actions by the United States has made the Pakistani army both more powerful within Pakistan and more antagonistic toward the United States.

Under current American policies, it is unlikely that American military relations with Pakistan will contribute positively in the near term to the Pakistani army's receptivity to greater democracy. Until things change, American military officials and officers in their relations with their Pakistani counterparts can only acknowledge the strong policy clashes of their governments and attempt to discuss informally with them the benefits of a true and functioning democracy for Pakistan and its armed forces.

Future events may change the policy picture, however. If the United States leaves Afghanistan and neutralizes the al Qaeda threat, then there might be an opportunity for turning a new leaf in U.S.-Pakistani military relations. As this develops, the United States should stop using military-military relationships for major national security issues and instead address these through regular government-government relationships. The United States should also reduce the importance of the intelligence relationship with Pakistan's military intelligence service (known as the Directorate for Inter-Services Intelligence, or ISI). In addition, U.S. policy should increase emphasis on Pakistan continuing its political development toward democracy. Under these conditions, interactions within normal military-military relations can resume the themes of the development of democracy and the armed forces' place and role in a democracy.

China

China is one of the most dynamic countries in the world. Its economic vigor is the most remarked upon aspect of the country by foreigners, but there is just as much change occurring within China's social structures and governmental systems. In addition, although the current emphasis on collective leadership is designed to minimize it, China has the ability to surprise. Therefore, in considering the potential for China to move toward democracy and the potential role of the People's Liberation Army (PLA) in that change, it is important to avoid extrapolating from today's conditions.

The current situation makes it difficult for foreign defense officials and military officers from democratic countries to make much headway with their counterparts in the PLA in promoting the merits of democratic systems. PLA officers are trained to consider the armed forces of democratic Taiwan, Japan, and the United States to be their enemies, bent on thwarting China's legitimate return to a powerful position in its region and the world. While they greatly admire American armed forces, in particular for their war-fighting prowess, and are eager to learn technical and tactical lessons, their admiration does not transfer to the democratic system of government that has created the American armed forces.

This handbook has repeated many times the observation that it is internal conditions that are decisive in a country's move toward or away from democracy, and this observation is very true in the case of China. One of the long-running and most important internal issues concerning the PLA has been its domestic mission. The Chinese regime is very clear that it is the ruling Chinese Communist Party, not the Chinese government, that directs the PLA. This concept dates back to the Chinese Civil War, when two parties, each with its own army, were fighting for control of China. However, this concept of the "party army" suffered a severe shock in 1989 in Tiananmen Square when the PLA was ordered out of the barracks not against a rival army but against protesting fellow citizens. It was every army's nightmare, to fire on its people rather than defend them, and the PLA did not relish the task. The Chinese government was concerned enough about the army's loyalty that it transferred military units from distant provinces to carry out the operation. After 1989 the PLA transferred a large number of personnel to the People's Armed Police and attempted also to transfer all responsibility for internal order. The party leadership agreed to assign the Ministry of the Interior primary responsibility for dealing with domestic protest and opposition but has insisted that the PLA remain the ultimate guarantor of the Chinese Communist Party's power and that it remain a party army.

The issue is still very much alive, however. Articles in the military media discuss the merits of the PLA becoming a national army despite the contrary official policy.[3] Such articles partly reflect the institutional self-interest for autonomy that all armies seek. A national army would have more autonomy than a party army, in which the Chinese Communist Party controls officer promotions and local party bosses give orders to local army units. However, the desire to be a national army also reflects the ethos of armed forces everywhere, to be and to be seen as defenders of the nation and protectors of its people.

The democracies and their military representatives who deal with the PLA should take every opportunity to encourage their counterparts to become a national army. Should it occur, this move will not result in any change in PLA suspicion and hostility toward the United States, Japan, and Taiwan. Nationalism runs deep in the PLA and has a xenophobic element that will not evaporate soon. However as national armed forces, the PLA will be much less likely to oppose democratic developments within China. As China realizes that political evolution toward democracy is necessary to sustain the economic and social development it needs, conservatives who oppose these trends will be less able to use the PLA to thwart progress.

Another area in which the democratic countries of the world that deal with China should continue to press for progress is in cooperation on common missions such as search and rescue, humanitarian response, maritime security, and peacekeeping operations. China itself is gradually increasing its participation in these activities as the PLA becomes more technically advanced and outward looking. Its number of personnel assigned to UN peacekeeping operations is still at a low level, but it has been steadily increasing. A small detachment of Chinese ships is in the Gulf of Aden, cooperating with the international operation against Somalia-based piracy. In most other countries, officers who serve overseas in international peace operations return to their home countries with a wider and more progressive attitude than their stay-at-home peers. The same will hold true for China, and other countries should welcome Chinese participation in conferences, training, exercises, and actual operations for the common good.

Finally, young Chinese officers should be invited to study at the military colleges of the democratic countries. Chinese military education is provincial in the literal sense: most Chinese officers in all services are educated in local military academies and have very little contact with the outside world until they reach senior rank. As discussed elsewhere in this handbook, a year in Australia, France, the United Kingdom, or the United States does not turn an officer from an autocratic country into a closet democrat, but it does open his or her eyes and mind to other possibilities.

8

The Challenge Ahead

As summarized in chapter 3 of this volume and detailed in volume 2, this handbook describes the successive waves of democratic transitions across the world, the crucial role that armed forces have played in those transitions, and the role of foreign military influences. Each democratic transition is unique. South Korea's and Taiwan's paths to democracy have been different from those of India, South Africa, Chile, or Poland. Often democratic development in a country has not proceeded uninterrupted in a single direction; there have been setbacks, even reversions to dictatorship, followed by new transitions. However, the overall trend clearly has been toward the expansion of democratic forms of government around the world.

Two of the most important factors in democratic transitions during the past half century have been the end of European colonial rule and the end of the cold war. Colonial rule was founded on military coercion and often ended by armed conflict; the cold war spurred high levels of military forces, intense superpower competition, and several proxy wars. These legacies and the power struggles when colonial rule and Soviet rule ended provided both opportunities for and obstacles to democratic development and often placed military forces at the center of governance change. On balance, the end of these eras boosted democratic development as the nondemocratic empires built on colonial and Leninist ideas crumbled. With these developments receding into the past, will there be a pause in the spread of democracy? Some scholars argue that in the wake of the cold war, a new form of government has emerged, "competitive authoritarianism," a hybrid of both democracy and authoritarianism that could persist for a long time.[1]

The experience of recent years suggests that the trend toward democracy will continue. The desire of individuals to govern their own affairs shows no sign of diminishing; rising living standards over time undermine dictators' claims that their regimes are essential for economic development; ever increasing personal contact and communication across national borders favors inspiration and collaboration. This trend was vividly illustrated in 2011 during the Arab Awakening, when events in one Arab country catalyzed actions in others within hours and days. Dictatorships in the twenty-first century are primarily

Chief of Naval Operations Adm. Gary Roughead meets with Egyptian army Field Marshal Mohamed Hussein Tantawi Soliman in 2009. (DoD photo by Mass Communication Specialist 1st Class Tiffini Jones Vanderwyst, U.S./Released)

motivated by a desire for power by the rulers, who rely on repression, delivering increased goods, or both to maintain power. The long-term advantages are with democracy. However, long-term advantages do not generate rapid or inevitable change. Both for their own security and to help those still living under oppression, the established democracies must support peaceful democratic development in those countries that have yet to achieve it. Military relations offer a powerful tool for this purpose.

There are a few basic ideas in this handbook. The first is that democracy is the best form of government for a country. Across all continents people have rejected dictatorship in favor of representative governments. Where dictatorships still persist, those leaders feel the need to pay lip service to democracy, cynically hijacking its vocabulary and subverting its forms. Democracies share common fundamental traits: the people choose their government through free elections, minorities and individuals have rights the government may not violate, power is shared by the executive and legislative branches, the press is open, and the courts are independent. Beyond these basic similarities there are many variations. Some have constitutional monarchs as head of state; others have presidents or prime ministers. The role of religion varies, and legal systems and codes take different forms.

The second basic idea is that democracies are best for the armed forces of a country. In democracies, the armed forces are generally more skilled, respected, and better paid than they are in dictatorships. Dictators often flatter and try to bribe their military leaders and units, but they also fear them, spy on them, and remove them if they become too powerful. Most important, a dictator will one day order his armed forces to use their weapons against their own people to keep him in power; the leader of an established democracy will never do so. It is therefore very much in the professional and personal self-interest of soldiers, sailors, and airmen to support a peaceful transition of their government from dictatorship to democracy.

The third basic idea is that the armed forces are one of the most important factors in the transition of a dictatorship to a democracy. While it is rare that the armed forces are the leaders of a democratic transition, they are nonetheless essential to its success. If they choose to support the dictator, he or she will remain in power, at least for a period of time. If they support democratic forces, or at a minimum do not oppose them, then democracy can succeed.

The fourth basic idea is that during their interactions with counterparts in dictatorships or in countries transitioning from authoritarian regimes, the servicemen and servicewomen from democratic countries can influence them to support, or at least not to oppose, transitions to democracy. The most important factors in a democratic transition are internal to a country, and the role that the armed forces of a country will play in a democratic transition is determined most strongly by its history, by the cohesion of the autocratic government and its ability to

During the Arab Awakening, Egyptians celebrate while riding on an army tank in Tahrir Square in January 2011. (RamyRaoof/Flickr)

deliver economic and social progress, by interactions among factions within the armed forces, and by the beliefs of individual military leaders. However, what they have observed and learned in dealing with foreign armed forces can affect their basic attitudes toward democracy and the role they choose to play in their country. What members of the military hear from foreign counterparts during political crises can influence where they decide to throw their support.

The fifth and final basic idea of this handbook is that the established democracies can do a better job of persuading military services in autocratic regimes to favor democratic transitions. The established democracies generally have welcomed the spread of democracy and encouraged democratic development as part of their policy goals. However, other national interests have often taken precedence—opposing the Soviet Union during the cold war, ensuring the flow of oil from the Persian Gulf, pursuing al Qaeda, and selling weapons systems—and democratic development was assigned lower importance than these other interests during the cultivation of individual bilateral relationships. Even when democratic development has been a priority, the established democracies have not thought of their defense and military relations as one of the effective means for supporting it. Military relations with autocratic regimes were directed toward developing the capability to operate together, relationships with senior military officers were used to gain support for immediate policy objectives, or military relationships were used as rewards and punishments for human rights behavior. These objectives for military relations have value, but none measures up to the long-term importance of encouraging the armed forces in an autocratic regime to support a peaceful transition of their country's form of governance to democracy.

For the future, the further spread of democracy around the world should be one of the overarching policy goals for the established democratic nations, and supporting democratic development should be one of the primary objectives of military relations with authoritarian or transitioning countries. As the prior chapters have shown, there are many ways in which military officers in their relationships with their counterparts in authoritarian countries can influence them to realize the advantages of a democratic system. If they are given the mission, the extremely capable officers, men, and women of the armed forces of the democracies will find even more effective ways to spread democratic ideals and practices.

Essential Elements of Intelligence Information Needed before Meeting with Counterparts in Authoritarian Countries

Before meeting with a senior officer from an autocratic country, a senior officer or defense official from a democratic country should understand the status of democratic development in that country, the various views and factions within the armed forces of that country, and the views of the counterpart with whom he or she is meeting. With this background knowledge, the officer from the democratic country can take advantage of opportunities to influence the counterpart officer or official in an effective manner.

History

What role did the armed forces play in the formation of the past and current governments of the country?

Civil-Military Power Relationships

How much authority and autonomy do the armed forces of the country have in the following areas:
> decisions to commit the armed forces to action;
> personnel promotions and assignments;
> legal treatment of members of the armed forces; and
> decisions to procure weapons systems?

Factions within the Armed Forces

What are the major factions within the armed forces?
Which senior officers and units belong to which faction?

Are factions based on individual leaders? On ethnicity, tribe, or religion?

What are the objectives of the factions: Self-preservation? Control of major military policy decisions? Reducing corruption? Democratic transition? Revenge?

Budgets

How are the armed forces of the country funded: Government budget? Business profits? Licenses? Shakedowns?

What are the pay levels for officers and enlisted personnel?

What is the compensation for officers and noncommissioned officers retiring from the service?

Do the armed forces run businesses? Which ones? How are the revenues used?

Corruption

What is the overall state of illegal payments at various levels of the armed forces?

Are there corrupt practices in military contracts for supplies and for equipment?

Which senior leaders are the most corrupt?

Individuals

Among the top military leadership, which leaders are the most likely to favor democratic change? Which are the most likely to oppose?

The Role of the Armed Forces in a Democratic System: Template for a War College or Regional Center Seminar

The topics and discussion questions cover the foundational elements of the armed forces in a democratic country. They are designed to cause officer-students to question these elements in their own countries and to learn from their fellow students about how different countries have established and maintain them.

Preparatory Reading

Chapters 2–4 of this handbook provide the best short introduction to the subject. The Further Reading at the end of this volume provide a more complete bibliography.

Seminar Discussion Topics and Questions

Constitutional and Legal Foundation of the Armed Forces

What are the strengths and limitations of different constitutional and legal foundations for the armed forces in different democracies around the world?

Case histories of countries with adequate constitutional and legal foundations for the armed forces but inadequate observance of the laws: the first three Nigerian republics and the Philippines. (See volume 2 of this handbook, chapters 11 and 8, respectively.)

Case histories of the role of military officers in different countries in establishing civil-military relations: General Gutierrez Mellado in Spain in the 1980s, General Vegh in Hungary in the 1990s, and General Nyanda in South Africa in the early

2000s). (See volume 2 of this handbook, chapters 16, 15, and 13, respectively.

What roles do legislatures play in overseeing the armed forces in different democracies around the world?

Mission

External defense: What are the procedures in various democracies to authorize the commitment of the armed forces to combat? Do military leaders have any responsibility to question an order to attack another country?

Internal operations: Under what circumstances and what rules are the armed forces authorized to take action against their own citizens? Are there democratic processes that govern these situations? Will soldiers be held accountable for their actions by current or future governments, and how can they ensure that their actions are justified?

International peacekeeping operations: When and why should a country commit units to international peacekeeping operations?

Case histories of senior military officers questioning the legality of orders from their government: General Angelo Reyes, Philippines chief of defense, during the EDSA II demonstrations of 2000; Tunisian general Rachid Ammar refusing the order of his president to fire on peaceful demonstrators in February 2011. (See volume 2 of this handbook, chapters 8 and 17, respectively.) The case of Michael Boyce, U.K. chief of defense staff at the start of the second Iraq war in 2003, is also instructive. (See chapter 2 in this volume.)

Case histories of internal operations in democracies: the British armed forces in Northern Ireland during the 1990s; the Indian armed forces in Kashmir in the early 2000s; the American military response to Hurricane Katrina in 2005.

Contribution to Society

Universal military service: What are the advantages and disadvantages of a volunteer versus a conscript force in a democracy? Is there any tension between the benefits for the country and the combat effectiveness of the armed forces?

Ethnic groups and minorities: How have different democracies around the world formed national armed forces from diverse population groups?

Do military veterans make better citizens when they leave the armed forces?

Case histories: General Diallo of Senegal in the 1960s; the Israeli and Singaporean experiences with conscription.

Political Neutrality

How do senior officers remain neutral when they are directed by their political superiors or approached by opposition leaders to provide political support?

How can military leaders inform the public about the effect of budget reductions while remaining politically neutral?

Case histories: civil-military relations during the 2001–06 Thaksin presidency; Australian chief of defense Admiral Barrie and the admission of homosexuals into the Australian armed forces in the 1990s; the 2003 petition signed by American retired senior officers to the Supreme Court when it was considering racial quotas in university admissions.

Ministries of Defense

Why is a strong and competent ministry of defense necessary in a democracy?

When a uniformed officer serves in a ministry of defense, does he sometimes have to take positions against the wishes of his own service?

Budgets, Pay, and Procurement

How is military pay determined in different democracies?

What are different safeguards against corruption in the awarding and fulfillment of military contracts?

Prestige, Reputation, and Rights

What rights does a service member forgo in different democracies that other citizens enjoy?

Should members of the armed forces, especially officers, be held
  to a higher standard of conduct than the population at large?
Should members of the armed forces be tried in military or civilian courts?

Field Trip Itineraries for Military Students from Autocratic and Transitional Countries

The purpose of these meetings is to introduce the full range of government agencies, other than the military, and nongovernmental groups that shape the role of the armed forces in democratic countries.

Legislative Branch

Meetings with
- ➤ elected members of the legislature who sit on armed forces committees, and members of their staffs;
- ➤ members of legislatures who have served in the armed forces.

Universities and Think Tanks

Meetings with
- ➤ military specialists in universities and in nonprofit think tanks;
- ➤ think tank specialists considered critical of the armed forces;
- ➤ military students in colleges and universities: Reserve Officer Training Corps undergraduate students; officers pursuing graduate degrees in civilian universities;
- ➤ sociologists, political scientists, and economists who study the role of the armed forces in society.

Media

Meetings with

- ➤ press and broadcast journalists reporting on military affairs;
- ➤ bloggers generally considered critical of the armed forces.

Veterans' Affairs Organizations

Meetings with

- ➤ officials from the government agencies responsible for providing health care and other services to veterans;
- ➤ staff and patients at veterans' hospitals and outpatient clinics;
- ➤ national and local chapters of organizations for veterans;
- ➤ organizations that support the armed forces, such as the Association of the U.S. Army and the Navy League of the United States.

Successful Ex-Servicemembers

Meetings with ex-servicemembers who have entered other professions after leaving the armed forces, for instance, in the realms of business, education, and government.

Exercise Checklist for the Legal and Democratic Use of Force

Every military exercise has a political-military context that is used as the basis for its simulated military operations. In a typical peacekeeping exercise, the participants assume that they are members of an international force patrolling a border area to enforce a cease-fire. Preparation of the scenario is a major component of the exercise planning process and should include establishment of the legal and democratic justification for the use of force. This aspect, as well as others shown below, should be discussed in seminars by the commanders and key staff members of all those participating in the exercise, not only in the planning phase but also during postexercise evaluations.

Legal Basis for the Objectives of the Military Forces in the Exercises

Authorization by the UN Security Council.
Acts of individual or collective self-defense.

Principle of Military Necessity

Military requirement for an action.
Assurance that the action does not violate the law of war.

Noncombatants

Principle of discrimination or distinction.
Only combatants or those participating directly in hostilities may lawfully be targeted—declarations of "hostile force."

Hors de combat (French for "outside the fight"): no targeting of prisoners, wounded, medical personnel, or journalists.

Civilians are to be protected unless they take a direct part in hostilities.

Defended and Undefended Places

Protected areas, hospitals, safety zones, and cultural properties.

Principle of Proportionality

Incidental loss of life and injury, collateral damage.

Taking precautions, judging commanders.

Ruses, Treachery, Perfidy, and Reprisals

Combatants concealing themselves among civilians.

Violation of truces.

Humanitarian Response

Relationship of military units to domestic agencies in the country; rules of engagement for dealing with looting or other lawless behavior in the affected area.

Notes

Chapter 1

1. For the military's role in the Chilean transition, see volume 2 of this handbook, chapter 4.

2. See volume 2, chapters 7 and 8, for more details on the process in Asia.

3. See chapters 17 and 18 in volume 2.

4. For South American examples, see Brian Loveman, *For La Patria* (Wilmington, Del.: Scholarly Resources, 1999).

5. For more details on the roles of individual military officers during transitions to democracy, see volume 2 of this handbook, chapters 4 (Chile), 8 (Philippines), 9 (Thailand), 12 (Senegal), 15 (Hungary), 16 (Spain), 17 (Middle East and North Africa), and 20 (Turkey).

6. See chapter 7 in this volume.

7. Freedom House, "Worst of the Worst 2012: The World's Most Repressive Societies" (www.freedomhouse.org/report/special-reports/worst-worst-2012-worlds-most-repressive-societies [December 2012]).

8. Ibid.

Chapter 2

1. Organization for Security and Cooperation in Europe, *Code of Conduct on Politico-Military Aspects of Security*, December 1994 (www.osce.org/fsc/41355 [November 2012]).

2. Ibid., p. 3.

3. "Democracy" has many meanings, and the term is often cynically misused. For the purposes of this handbook, a democracy is a nation in which government leaders are chosen by free and fair elections; policies are made by majority decision, but minorities are protected; and the basic freedoms of individuals and of institutions like the press are protected by laws and an independent judicial system.

4. See volume 2 of this handbook, chapter 16.

5. For more details on the situation in Chile, see volume 2, chapter 4.

6. See volume 2, chapter 8.

7. See volume 2, chapter 7.

8. Chapters 5, 12, and 13 of volume 2 provide more information on this topic for El Salvador, Senegal, and South Africa, respectively.

9. See volume 2, chapter 9.

10. For more details, see volume 2, chapter 15.

Chapter 3

1. See volume 2 of this handbook, chapter 14 for a fuller discussion of the role of the military in Europe and Eurasia.

2. For the situation in Hungary, see chapter 15 of volume 2.

3. See volume 2, chapter 2.

4. The cases of Argentina and Chile are covered in more detail in chapters 3 and 4, respectively, of volume 2.

5. See volume 2, chapter 6.

6. For more details on the military's response in Indonesia, see volume 2, chapter 7.

7. More information on the case of sub-Saharan Africa is provided in volume 2, chapter 10.

8. For a more detailed exploration of the role of the military in the Middle East and North Africa, see volume 2, chapter 17; for details on Turkey, see volume 2, chapter 20.

Chapter 4

1. See volume 2 of this handbook, chapter 20.

2. Sarah El Deeb, "Egypt's Ruling Generals Defend Their Businesses," Associated Press, March 28, 2012 (www.guardian.co.uk/world/feedarticle/10168470).

Chapter 5

1. OECD, *OECD DAC Handbook on Security System Reform (SSR): Supporting Security and Justice* (Paris, 2007).

2. Ibid., p. 21.

3. White House, *National Security Strategy* (May 2010), p. 37.

4. For an exhaustive description of many of the American programs, see U.S. Department of Defense and U.S. Department of State, *Foreign Military Training, Fiscal Years 2009 and 2010. Joint Report to Congress,* vol. 1 (www.state.gov/t/pm/rls/rpt/fmtrpt/2010/index. htm [November 2012]).

5. U.S. Department of State, Bureau of Political-Military Affairs, *Foreign Military Training and DoD Engagement Activities of Interest: Joint Report to Congress,* March 2002 (www.state.gov/t/pm/rls/rpt/ fmtrpt/2002/10607.htm [December 2012]).

Chapter 6

1. For an overview of the Freedom House study and data, see Adrian Karatnycky and Peter Ackerman, "How Freedom Is Won: From Civic Resistance to Durable Democracy," *International Journal of Not-for-Profit Law* 7, no. 3 (2005) (www.icnl.org/research/journal/ vol7iss3/special_3.htm [December 2012]).

2. Erica Chenoweth and Maria Stephan, *Why Civil Resistance Works: The Strategic Logic of Nonviolent Conflict* (Columbia University Press, 2011), p. 9.

3. *The U.S. Army/U.S. Marine Corps Counterinsurgency Field Manual* (University of Chicago Press, 2007), p. 37.

4. Ibid., p. 38.

5. Ibid., p. 221.

6. Chenoweth and Stephan, *Why Civil Resistance Works.*

Chapter 7

1. See New Mandala, *Constitution of the Republic of the Union of Myanmar,* September 2008 (http://asiapacific.anu.edu.au/new mandala/wp-content/uploads/2009/01/myanmar_constitution-2008- en.pdf [December 2012]), p. 3.

2. Raymond Maalouf, "Kingdom of Saudi Arabia: A Case Study," unpublished paper written for the Council for a Community of Democracies, January 20, 2012.

3. David Shambaugh, "Civil-Military Relations in China: Party-Army or National Military?" *Copenhagen Journal of Asian Studies* 16 (2002): 10–29 (ej.lib.cbs.dk/index.php/cjas/article/download/3/3 [December 2012]).

Chapter 8

1. Steven Levitsky and Lucan A. Way, *Competitive Authoritarianism: Hybrid Regimes after the Cold War* (Cambridge University Press, 2010).

Further Reading

Democracy

Freedom House. 2013. *Freedom in the World 2013* (www.freedom house.org/sites/default/files/FIW%202013%20Booklet%20-%20 for%web.pdf).

For the last forty years, using a consistent set of standards, Freedom House has been publishing detailed ratings of political rights and civil liberties in all countries in the world. Political rights and civil liberties are the foundational elements of democracy, and countries that rank high on the Freedom House scale are democracies while those that rank low are dictatorships. This annual survey is the most authoritative statement on the state of democracy in the world.

Kinsman, Jeremy, and Kurt Bassuener. 2008. *A Diplomat's Handbook for Democracy Development Support* (www.diplomatshandbook.org).

A companion and earlier piece to this handbook, the *Diplomat's Handbook* provides practical recommendations to the ambassadors of the established democracies and their staffs on how to support democratic development in the countries where they are stationed. It also provides case histories and historical examples of diplomatic action in supporting democracy.

Levitsky, Steven, and Lucan A. Way. 2012. *Competitive Authoritarianism: Hybrid Regimes after the Cold War*. Cambridge University Press.

Two political scientists argue that a new form of government has emerged following the cold war that combines elections with abuses of power by incumbent leaders and that such regimes have demonstrated staying power in many countries. The book is heavy on political theory but also contains a wealth of detail and insight on individual countries. Levitsky and Way show that in those countries where linkage to Western nations was the strongest, democratic transitions were more likely to occur.

Palmer, Mark. 2003. *Breaking the Real Axis of Evil: How to Oust the World's Last Dictators by 2025.* Lanham, Md.: Rowman and Littlefield.

Ambassador Mark Palmer has been the most effective and influential American promoter of democracy worldwide. This book both tells the story of what has been accomplished in the growth of democracy, lays out the challenge for the future, and gives a comprehensive and imaginative description of the tools that can be brought to bear by the established democracies in support of democratic development worldwide.

Civil-Military Relations

Barany, Zoltan. 2012. *The Soldier and the Changing State: Building Democratic Armies in Africa, Asia, Europe and the Americas.* Princeton University Press.

This recent book by a University of Texas scholar describes the role the armed forces have played in twenty-seven post–World War II case studies of democratization, including some that are also covered in the fourteen case studies in volume 2 of this handbook. Barany's objective is to identify the military factors that make for successful or unsuccessful democratic transitions. Unlike this handbook, he does not concentrate on the role of outside influences, but there are many interesting and useful insights in his accounts.

Huntington, Samuel P. 1957. *The Soldier and the State: The Theory and Politics of Civil-Military Relations.* Belknap/Harvard University Press.

Harvard professor Huntington traces the military profession from ancient times, discusses the cases of the German and Japanese officer corps through World War II, then describes civil-military roles in the United States through the cold war. While dated and United States centric, this remains the classic text of civil-military relations.

Janowitz, Morris. 1960. *The Professional Soldier: A Social and Political Portrait.* Glencoe, Ill.: Free Press.

Janowitz, a University of Michigan professor, wrote this classic book on civil-military relations based on hundreds of interviews with American military officers. His model of civil-military relations is sophisticated, reflecting the interactions of politics, technology, and war that blurred sharp lines between the military profession, the rest of government, and American society. It reflects the American and cold war environment in which it was written, but the issues it addresses are relevant to every country and military organization.

Organization for Security and Cooperation in Europe. 1994. "Code of Conduct on Politico-Military Aspects of Security" (www.osce.org/fsc/41355).

This document was adopted at the Ninety-First Plenary Meeting of the Special Committee of the Conference on Security and Cooperation in Europe in Budapest in December 1994. It provides roughly thirty principles that cover the full range of how armed forces in democratic countries should be organized, authorized, controlled, and employed.

Security System Reform

Security system reform (SSR) is the series of actions that developing democracies take to establish effective and appropriate roles and controls for their armed forces, police forces, and intelligence organizations. Both outside countries and nongovernmental organizations often provide SSR assistance to developing democracies at their request.

NATO. 2008. *Partnership Action Plan on Defense Institution Building Reference Curriculum: Public Administration and Governance, Defense Management and Economics, Ethics and Leadership* (www.nato.int/nato_static/assets/pdf/.../20090908_PAB-DIB_en.pdf).

This book, compiled by representatives from many NATO defense colleges, provides curriculum modules for the education of both defense officials and military officers in democratizing countries.

Organization for Economic Cooperation and Development (OECD), Development Assistance Committee. 2005. *Security System Reform and Governance: A DAC Reference Document.* Paris.

The OECD is a group of thirty democracies cooperating on a full range of economic, social, and environmental challenges. This book describes the purposes and categories of SSR and includes several essays on the state of OECD SSR efforts around the world.

OECD. 2007. *The OECD DAC Handbook on Security System Reform (SSR): Supporting Security and Justice*. Paris.

This very practical handbook outlines seven steps in SSR, from "establishing the basic principles for security and justice system reforms" through "implementing SSR sector by sector" to "managing international assistance programmes." Written by a team of SSR experts from around the world, it is filled with practical examples, lists of questions to address, and lessons learned from international practice.

Civil Resistance

Binnendijk, Anika Locke, and Ivan Marovic. 2006. "Power and Persuasion: Nonviolent Strategies to Influence State Security Forces in Serbia (2000) and Ukraine (2004)." *Communist and Post Communist Studies* 39 (3): 411–29.

This article gives a detailed account of the tactics used by Serbian and Ukrainian resistance movements to convince the armed forces not to suppress popular demonstrations that overthrew dictators in both regimes.

Chenoweth, Erica, and Maria J. Stephan. 2011. *Why Civil Resistance Works: The Strategic Logic of Nonviolent Conflict*. Columbia University Press.

Two scholars of civil resistance explain how both armed insurrection and nonviolent civil resistance have been successful in overthrowing authoritarian regimes and establishing democratic governments since 1900. The data support civil resistance as the more effective path. The authors reported their findings in an earlier article of the same title in *International Security*, volume 33, number 1 (Summer 2008).

Index